# SMALL TALK TECHNIQUES

# SMALL TALK

## TECHNIQUES

## SMART STRATEGIES
### for Personal and Professional Success

Lisa Chau

ROCKRIDGE
PRESS

For general information on our other products and services or to obtain technical support, please contact our Customer Care Department within the United States at (866) 744-2665, or outside the United States at (510) 253-0500.

Rockridge Press publishes its books in a variety of electronic and print formats. Some content that appears in print may not be available in electronic books, and vice versa.

Interior and Cover Designer: Stephanie Sumulong
Art Producer: Tom Hood
Editors: Brian Sweeting and John Makowski
Production Editor: Matt Burnett
Cover and interior illustrations courtesy Palto/iStock.

ISBN: Print 978-1-64739-984-9 | eBook 978-1-64739-985-6

R0

This book is dedicated to the people who patiently supported me on the journey to writing it. I thank my Dartmouth College family and offer my gratitude to the Tuck School of Business for serving as the springboard for my writing career.

# CONTENTS

# INTRODUCTION

I embrace small talk as an integral part of life, because the better I've become at this skill, the greater gains I've seen in my personal and professional life. Engaging in small talk creates opportunities to connect with others in meaningful exchanges. It has helped me learn new information, grow my community, get invited to private functions, get job interviews, get dates . . . It's uplifting, and it's an act of kindness.

Small talk has become an important part of my life, and it is something I practice as much as possible.

Unless you're a hermit, you will likely encounter small talk on a regular basis. It's an inescapable facet of daily life. Introverts, extroverts, and everyone in between partake in this social practice.

"I haven't gone golfing in over a week."

"That's a really fun dinosaur shirt you're wearing."

"The forecast predicts another sunny day."

Maybe you have no interest in golf, you can't figure out why your choice in clothing has any relevance to the person speaking to you, and you already know it's going to be sunny for the rest of the week. Out of politeness, you will respond with a comment that may seem equally trivial. Sometimes, small talk will lead to deeper discussions with plans to speak or meet again. Other times, you will never see the person again. Realistically, there are people you will see and chit-chat with repeatedly but never invite to dinner at your home.

If you're keeping score, the number of times you engage in small talk will lead to noteworthy results less than half of the time. You could say that it's an inefficient activity.

Yet, you cannot avoid small talk. It's at the grocery store, the gym, and the airport. Even when we are paid employees on the clock, almost every meeting and conference call begins with small talk.

"My brother took his son to the new playground on 80th Street."

"I finally watched that football documentary you've all been raving about."

"Hear me out: Seasoned kale chips in the kitchen pantry!"

As much as I love kale chips, I am fairly certain they won't be the catalyst for transforming a mediocre project into an award-winning one. On the surface, small talk may seem like a waste of time. The comments are irrelevant to the task at hand or don't produce profits.

Below the surface, however, small talk can lead to extremely meaningful friendships, and yes, even land large accounts. While inefficient, our social habit has the power to build trust over time. You need to look at the long-term value of small talk rather than for immediate results. Small talk is a verbal handshake that signals others to engage with us in conversation that may lead to more.

I hated small talk until several years after I graduated college. It's only when I changed my mindset to be more open and curious about others that I began to embrace it. I've spent the last decade honing this skill as a part of my professional and personal development. I'm happier and more successful for it.

For example, at a Yale alumni event over five years ago, I stayed long after most other guests had left—so much later that the coat room had already been locked up with my belongings trapped in it. While I was looking for someone to help me, I started a conversation with Lou Martarano. That's when I learned about the Yale Alumni Nonprofit Alliance (YANA). Soon after, I was introduced to the Founding Chair Ken Inadomi and invited to join the group. As a result, I've met many wonderful people in the social impact space.

In this book, I'm sharing small-talk strategies that will serve you well no matter your personality or stage in life. You'll learn how to establish rapport, engage your whole body, and prepare for an event, among many other skills. These are easy yet invaluable tips to help anyone improve the way they relate to and engage with others.

## CHAPTER ONE

# OPEN UP

Small talk is a social practice ubiquitous in our daily lives. We encounter it in personal and professional settings: the cafe, the salon, the office, the airport . . . the list of scenarios is endless. We use it to establish connections with strangers, friends, and colleagues.

Small talk can add a spark to your otherwise mundane commute, or it can eventually help you land a large account at work. Maybe your cheery disposition will mean a free muffin with your coffee order, or maybe it means you meet your best friend the next time you chat with a stranger. Small talk can lead to all sorts of unexpected results, but ultimately, it is used to develop rapport—whether fleeting or longer term. Over time, it creates trust, or at least credibility. Use small talk as a verbal handshake to welcome others into an interaction for further engagement.

# Get Ready to Talk

Whether you're anxious about engaging in small talk or you're someone who enjoys it, everyone can improve their skills and pick up some new tips. Good small-talk skills can lead to new information, new friends, or new professional contacts and resources. They foster closer relationships and positive reputations.

I've learned so much via small talk. It may start out completely generic, but leading questions can pave the road to new knowledge.

Maybe you'll learn about a new workshop:

> "Oh, I'm also a baker. Have you ever attended the workshops at the culinary school across town? I'm wondering which ones I should register to take in the evenings."

> "Yes! I highly recommend the French bread series. The instructors are the best! They're patient and attentive."

Maybe you'll be offered a service you weren't seeking:

> "My assistant is leaving in the fall to get her MBA in California. Do you know if anyone is looking for a role working in textiles?"

> "No, but my friend is the head of career services for the local community college. Would you like her to post your job opening in their database?"

Always be ready to talk. It's a win even if it just puts a smile on your face for the day.

# Keep an Open Mind

It is incredibly easy to judge someone based on their appearance. Our brains do this automatically. In a *Forbes* article, Serenity Gibbons explained that people form a solid opinion of you within the first seven seconds of meeting. She notes that some studies even suggest that we make judgments about character and trustworthiness in a mere tenth of a second!

While many will tell you to trust your gut reactions—and while you will involuntarily judge people upon first impression based on vocal inflection, attractiveness, general emotional state, etc.—I advise you not to let these initial impressions determine whether or not you will speak with someone.

Even if you're presented with evidence to the contrary of your initial judgment, it may still be difficult to discard your prejudices, but try. It could lead to the beginning of a wonderful unexpected friendship. Years ago, at an alumni holiday party, I met a couple that I was certain would hate me. Today, I've taken long train rides to attend the husband's annual birthday parties on their estate. I've been to their homes on multiple occasions and have an open invite to visit. They are extremely generous to me and any friends I bring along.

## You Never Know Who You Might Meet

Some events bring together people from all walks of life: sporting events, music festivals, comic book conventions. People who might never have met during their daily routines will cross paths at such gatherings. A sous chef might meet a pilot. A foreign exchange student might meet a cow farmer. The combinations are infinite and can have infinite results.

Take, for instance, the homeschooling mother who was carrying a bag printed with her child's painting. While in line for hot dogs, a Fortune 500 marketing executive asked about

→

the artwork. They chatted for 10 minutes before getting their food. A business card was offered, and two months later, the child's painting was bought for $2,000 and used in national commercials for sneakers.

# Be Empathetic

Keep in mind that a lot of people don't like small talk. My former self eschewed it. I internally eyerolled whenever it was forced on me. Even those who aren't annoyed by small talk might dread it or experience anxiety around the experience. While I've learned to embrace small talk as a strategy and even enjoy it, I still experience anxiety. I mentally stress over whether people will allow their first impression to decide if they will speak with me. I worry that I won't come across as articulate because I will forget the words I need to express myself coherently. If you relate to any of these examples or know you have social anxiety, rest assured that others do as well. Even the most extroverted person might wonder if they arrived in the appropriate shoes.

> Be empathetic to yourself and be empathetic to others. Often, it takes time for a conversation to become natural.

Be empathetic to yourself and be empathetic to others. Often, it takes time for a conversation to become natural. Rapport isn't always immediate. People have different timelines for when they will trust others. Remember to be flexible in how you approach others or welcome them into your personal space. You're not the only one who may feel anxious. As much as you feel judged by others, they may feel the same or moreso.

# Be Kind

Even the nicest people will have bad days or days where they're simply exhausted. We never know what others are dealing with in their lives, how they're feeling, or how their day has unfolded. We don't have the luxury of choosing the circumstances of our existence. Be kind.

During graduate school at Dartmouth College, I took a road trip with a fellow student from Hanover, New Hampshire, to Virginia and back. She told me that toll collectors have some of the highest rates of depression and that we should make a point to say at least seven words to each one we encountered. She explained that seven words is the minimum for making a person feel you are giving them your attention. Toll booth operators work in inhumane conditions and rarely feel as if drivers respect them or their profession. We made a point to try changing that with seven words and maybe brighten their day, if only for a moment. We refused to judge people's value by their profession. All honest work deserves respect.

# Value Your Contribution

One of the most important lessons I teach during workshops or keynote speeches is to always add value. I invite you to think about what you have to contribute to a conversation. What can you offer in terms of experience, skills, personality, talent, or knowledge? You don't want to show up with nothing to give. Don't be a taker, be a giver.

Be excited to share the details of your life in a meaningful way. Are you passionate about your job? Are you passionate about a hobby? What makes you interesting, and where is the overlap between you and your conversation partner? Do you get excited about the same things? Mutual interests can form instant bonds, while different hobbies can ignite curiosity for further discussion.

Think about how you can serve as a resource for someone else. What can you teach another person? As an exercise, list out the best attributes you have to offer others and how you would convey them in a conversation.

Maybe you have a great sense of humor and you will bring levity to another person's day. Who doesn't love a great joke?

Maybe you have quick problem-solving skills and you can help someone else brainstorm a solution for something that's gotten them stuck.

Offer valuable contributions and people will seek to speak with you again.

# Visualize It

Small talk does not come easily to everyone. Practicing on your own can help alleviate the anxiety that comes with speaking to others. Try imagining yourself having the conversations provided throughout this book and practicing the tips. Visualize yourself in the scenarios I've provided as examples.

Notice which types of conversations come easily and which require more effort. Use a mirror to consider your facial expressions, how you hold your body, and if you react appropriately. Don't worry if this seems unnatural. You will feel self-conscious. The feeling will subside over time.

In the beginning, be yourself in your visualizations. How would you start a conversation? What are topics you enjoy speaking about? How would you convey the best attributes you have to offer others?

After you gain a little confidence in your presentation, you can try pretending to be the people you expect to engage. Ask yourself why others would want to speak with you. How would they form their first impression of you? What questions would they ask you? Why would they want to speak with you again?

# Remember This

- Being good at small talk takes practice and time. Don't worry if improvement is not immediate. It will come with the effort you invest.

- Know your worth and always add value. Be ready to contribute to conversations with insight, humor, and resources. Offer before you take.

- Keep an open mind and be empathetic. Don't allow your first impressions to determine who you choose to engage in a discussion. You might be pleasantly surprised!

CHAPTER TWO

# ENGAGE YOUR BODY

First impressions are very important. They are extremely difficult to change once formed, especially if a person is not open-minded. Our brains automatically make judgments about other people in a matter of seconds—sometimes even before anything is said!

So, it is prudent to consider how you present yourself as well as what you say. Body language can speak louder than words, and it can be used to make people feel at ease and comfortable. Carry yourself with confidence, but be approachable. Avoid being overly stiff or overly relaxed. Welcome someone into conversation with a genuine smile.

# Practice Good Body Language and Posture

You should always be mindful of your presence. What is your body language conveying about you to others? Remember, our brains can subconsciously detect subtle cues and changes in others' expressions and bodies.

Correcting poor posture habits will improve the confidence that you exude. Keep your shoulders back, and imagine an invisible string pulling through the core of your torso through the top of your head. Be careful not to come across as stiff, as that will render everyone uncomfortable. You need to be in control of your body, but hold it naturally and slightly relaxed.

Avoid crossing your arms because it appears defensive. You're closing yourself off physically and mentally. You may also look stubborn or angry. Instead, keep your arms down by your sides, with your palms facing the other person. This signals to the other person that you are open and not hiding anything.

It's always good to keep your hands in view of the other person. This makes it easier for them to trust you. It's why you don't want to clasp your hands behind your body where they can't be seen. Try not to provoke apprehension, discomfort, or displeasure.

Body language can be extremely powerful, so you should practice what you are trying to convey. You are aiming to be welcoming and approachable. You should confidently provide a sense of comfort and trustworthiness.

# Mirror Expressions

Have you ever watched people who really enjoy speaking with one another? They will subconsciously mirror each other's gestures and poses. If one person crosses their legs, the other will soon follow, and their bodies will be pointed toward each other.

If Jeremy takes a sip of his drink, Juan will likely take a sip of his own soon after.

If Varin touches her chin, Michael will also reach for his own face.

Mimicking the body language of the person you're speaking with forms a subconscious bond and comfortability between you. It's like your bodies are demonstrating that you're on the same wavelength and that you're forming a nonverbal rapport. Many times, I find myself mirroring my conversation partner without even thinking about it. It naturally happens, unplanned.

> Mimicking the body language of the person you're speaking with forms a subconscious bond and comfortability between you.

Of course, it's great if your body unconsciously syncs with the other person's without either of you noticing. Since that's not always the case, you can purposely choose to adopt the other person's body language. However, you want to do this inconspicuously!

You must be subtle or you will come across as creepy. Don't imitate every movement. Avoid copying exactly and immediately. Do a slight variation and let some time pass before you mirror any gesture.

## Smile Appropriately

I was born and raised in New York City. We're taught early on that smiling is not cool and it makes you look vulnerable. In fact, if you go around smiling at everyone, people will think you're either strange or a tourist, or both. We are not an outwardly friendly bunch.

When I left Manhattan to attend Wellesley College, I brought my attitude with me. I spent my weekends off-campus, partying at Harvard and MIT. Few strangers tried striking up conversations with me during my first and second years. Puzzled, I asked friends why no one tried chatting with me. They replied by telling me that I looked unapproachable, bordering on mean. As much as I found this hilarious, I started dressing more casually and I smiled more. More people started talking to me because my smiling was a signal that I was open to engagement. There was little risk of immediate rejection. I was approachable.

Not all smiles are equal, however. Your smile needs to be authentic. There have been times when I forced my smile and it scared people away. I looked creepy or unnatural.

Genuine smiles involve the entire face. A relaxed expression forms the backdrop for upturned corners of the lips and crinkles by the side of the eyes. The brain can quickly sense a real smile from a fake one by recognizing these details.

Even if your smile is authentic, it would be odd for it to be permanently plastered on your face. Be mindful to grin appropriately. You should definitely smile when you want to invite someone into a conversation or to show that you're happy. In conversation, it's best to wait for relevant times to flash a smile.

# Make Eye Contact

Eyes are very important for communication. They may also be a source of great anxiety if you do not know how to balance the right amount of eye contact. You always want to look into the other person's eyes just enough to communicate that you are friendly, inviting, and attentive. Too little eye contact seems shifty, shy, or disinterested, but too much makes one seem awkward, intense, or aggressive.

I really like the tips the writer Arlin Cuncic provides for how and when to make eye contact:

- Meet eyes with someone before you initiate conversation.

- When you're speaking, maintain eye contact 50 percent of the time.

- When you're listening, maintain eye contact 70 percent of the time.

- Keep eye movements slow. Avoid darting your eyes.

- Break eye contact after about four seconds to look at another part of their face briefly.

- Every so often, nod or gesture when you've broken your gaze.

In group settings, make sure you make eye contact with everyone individually. Switch who you're focused on with each new idea or after every two to three sentences. Try to be inclusive and give everyone attention.

If someone is not returning your eye contact, try asking them a direct question. At a minimum, by asking them a question, you fully engage them in the discussion.

## What Not to Do

I have gone to hundreds of business and social events over the past decade. Last year, I witnessed some of the most off-putting behavior at a networking event held at the end of summer. A bedraggled young man arrived late to the presentation but insisted on choosing a seat in the fourth row, which required five other guests to get up for him. After he finally sat down in his chair, he made a big production of pulling out half the contents of his backpack to reach his laptop—not to take notes, but to check his email and play on Facebook.

In a sea of dark suits and ties, the man stood out like a sore thumb in a wrinkled and brightly colored Hawaiian shirt more appropriate for a day at the beach. His choice of attire signaled to others that he either did not understand the situation or did not respect the host enough to dress in an acceptable manner. His blatant lack of attention during the presentation further signaled his boredom and disinterest in the event.

Once the speaker finished her question-and-answer session, the man popped out of his seat and hurriedly pushed his way to the reception area where he gathered massive amounts of hot food. He chose a small, remote table where he

→

sat down with his plate before splaying the rest of his belongings around him. There was no room for anyone else to join him, but I doubt anyone would have wanted to. He chewed with his mouth open while intently gazing into his computer screen. When he was done eating, he conducted a loud phone call to confirm weekend brunch plans before leaving.

No one spoke to him or even tried. Why would they? What would they have gained from any conversation with that person?

# Use Your Hands

My mother tried to mold me into an elegant young lady who speaks in soft tones and gracefully moves in delicate, slight motions. If you knew me, you'd be laughing right now. Thanks to mandatory communications and theater classes at Hunter High School, augmented by years with the debate team, I am an assertive speaker who projects her voice. I also punctuate my statements with my hands.

While it's not advisable to go flailing your arms and hands around onstage or off, using your hands while you speak is recommended. Some professors will often use body language to emphasize important points in the classroom. When people actively gesture while they are communicating, they are perceived as energetic and charismatic. In contrast, those who don't gesture much while they talk come across as distant and wooden.

In the *Washington Post* article "What to Do with Your Hands When Speaking in Public," Vanessa Van Edwards explains, "When really charismatic leaders use hand gestures, the brain is super happy because it's getting two explanations in one, and the brain loves that."

In a controlled manner, try highlighting important points by waving a hand in the air while you're speaking, no more than half the distance between you and the other person. For extra emphasis, fan out your hands from the elbows with your palms open. When mentioning numbers under five, show the same number of fingers to help people remember.

Avoid aggressive gestures. You don't want to chop the air or pound your fist. Pointing is also usually frowned upon by experts.

## Balance Food and Drink

I'm not going to lie; I love food. I've definitely attended events where the food was the only redeeming quality. That said, if you're going to an event, it should be to connect with others. I'm not telling you, as one of my supervisors told me, not to eat or drink anything. However, you should practice both in moderation. Don't be gluttonous and don't get drunk.

I've never been to an event where less than 85 percent of the guests were eating or drinking. So, I suggest that you carry at least a glass of water with you. I've found that others get self-conscious about their hors d'oeuvres and wine if I'm completely empty-handed.

It should go without saying that speaking with your mouth full is rude. Don't do it. If you're eating, do so when the other person is talking. If you're asked a question, finish chewing before you answer. Take small, manageable bites and sips. Again, you're there to meet other people, not to have dinner.

Nonetheless, having food with others is a great bonding ritual. Plus, it gives you really great conversation starters because it's visual, available, and most people have opinions about food. It's usually a fairly safe topic to discuss.

## Don't Fidget

If you're anxious about speaking with someone, it's common to fidget. It's also noticeable when people are bored or letting their minds wander while something else is happening in front of them. Common fidgeting behaviors include playing with your hair, fingers, or nearby objects such as pens, drinking glasses, or mobile phones. Some people may also move around awkwardly, drum their fingers, or wag their foot.

You really want to keep fidgeting to a minimum, if not completely absent. When you fidget, it conveys to the other person that you are disinterested, nervous, or impatient. It's a blockage to the connection you're trying to develop, and you may make the other person uncomfortable and distrustful of you.

Some methods which may help you avoid distraction include reducing your caffeine and sugar intake—in general, but especially before and during events. Also try to increase your exercise regimen and add relaxation and meditation techniques to your daily life.

Ultimately, the best way to avoid fidgeting is to focus on what the other person is saying. If you only have the least bit of interest in the topic, either ask deeper dive questions that require thought or change the subject. There is nothing to be gained if you present yourself like a trapped animal simply because you don't want to be in a conversation.

# Look Engaged

We've all been in conversations where the other person looked bored and like they wanted to escape. You should never be that person. You must take responsibility for the success of any interaction. What are you contributing and doing to make the discussion a success?

First, put away your phone. It is the most common distraction in any event I've attended. Hide it out of view so you can't see, hear, or feel the temptation to check it. No blinking lights, no ringing, no vibrations. Gone. Show that you are committed to the present moment and that the other person has your full attention.

Next, listen. Listen so you can demonstrate understanding by paraphrasing parts of the conversation back to the other person. Focus on what they are saying. Ask relevant questions to get deeper into the topic. Do not listen just so you can immediately formulate a counterpoint. You're not trying to dominate a debate. You're cultivating a pleasant exchange of ideas.

Body language is also useful in showing that you are engaged in a discussion. Nod your head to agree every so often. Raise your eyebrows to convey surprise or curiosity. Smile. Maintain eye contact. Occasionally, and subtly, mirror their gestures. Keep yourself engaged in a way that fosters positive conversation.

## Remember This

- Maintain a good balance of eye contact.

- Subtly mirror gestures and expressions.

- Practice good posture and hold your body with confidence.

The more you practice, the more these motions will become second nature to you. Try practicing in front of a mirror, and then with trusted friends. You'll get there.

## CHAPTER THREE

# START STRONG

The window of opportunity for you to make a strong first impression is very small but extremely important, because it sets the tone for the rest of the interaction (and beyond). Clear your head so you can be committed to being fully present for the other person. Gracefully enter the conversation with a welcoming introduction and be positive. Having a sunny disposition will start the discussion off on the right foot and pave the way for the rest of the exchange.

If you are meeting others in person, be mindful of your appearance because people will see you even before anything is said. Use your posture to convey confidence and your smile to welcome further interaction. Extend your hand for a firm handshake and introduce yourself by name while maintaining eye contact.

I often like to make a comment about the event where I'm meeting the other person and follow with an invite for them to share their thoughts. I might ask what brings them to the event, how they enjoyed it so far, or what they're looking forward to next.

# Be Prepared

When done well, small talk is a powerful personal and professional strategy. It strengthens interpersonal bonding, builds rapport, and cultivates trust. Far from being a waste of time, it sets the foundation for a lasting impression. The most successful people learn to use small talk as a way to open doors and create significant opportunities that might not have otherwise been available.

Although the ability to connect with others is often categorized as a soft skill that lacks rigorous training, it's quite the opposite. As Amy Blaschka wrote in *Forbes* last year, "there is nothing easy about soft skills; in many cases, they can be harder to master and take more practice to achieve than technical knowledge." In fact, current President of Dartmouth College Philip J. Hanlon more accurately describes relationship building as a "power skill."

> The most successful people learn to use small talk as a way to open doors and create significant opportunities that might not have otherwise been available.

There are two parts to preparing for effective small talk: research and preparing your mindset.

# Research

Even before you speak with anyone, you should at least investigate and review the basics before going into a meeting or a networking event. For example:

1.  Who will you be speaking with and what can you offer one another?

2.  How do you know this person? Is this a first-time meeting or do you have a history? If the latter, refresh yourself on prior conversations you've had together.

3.  What are your specific goals? Are you trying to raise funding for your start-up or join the board of the local charity organization?

# Prepare Your Mindset

You need to place yourself in the appropriate mindset to have a conversation that yields fruitful results. For example:

1.  Be present. Don't let distractions draw your attention elsewhere.

2.  Have a positive attitude. If you engage in small talk thinking it's a waste of time, you've already made it a waste of time. It's a self-fulfilling prophesy.

3.  Keep your interest in the other person. Be curious about others.

Successful small talk really relies on solid preparation and practice. Always be prepared to mold the chance to create a good impression while setting the tone for your interaction.

# Preparation Improves Presentation

Jennifer was extremely nervous about introducing herself to a bestselling author. She was a reporter for her university newspaper and usually wrote culture critiques.

She glanced over to see that three young fans remained in line to get the author's signature and photo. Jennifer pulled back her shoulders, took two deep breaths, and gave her appearance one last check using the reflection in the window. She closed her eyes to review the details about the author she had researched and memorized the previous night. Then, she focused her sights on the author. In her mind, she practiced the first three things she wanted to say. Finally, she purposely walked across the room to the signing table with a relaxed smile on her face.

When Jennifer stood across from the author, she extended her hand and introduced herself in a clear, steady voice, "Good evening, Mr. D'Amato. My name is Jennifer Richter and I'm a huge fan who has read all your novels. I just started reading your mother Barbara's murder mysteries, and I would love to interview you about the lessons you learned from her."

To Jennifer's delight, the author agreed to the interview after they talked for another 20 minutes.

# Anticipate Questions

One of the best ways to train yourself to master small talk is anticipating questions. People will often ask common questions that you are able to easily respond to since you already know to expect them. Just try not to sound bored or rehearsed when you're invited to chat about the weather or your weekend for the twentieth time.

Of course, the most common question in the United States is, "What do you do (for a living)?" If this is not the very first question asked, it usually happens very early on in the conversation. I have found this to be a pivotal moment, where you either draw in the other person or completely lose them. The challenge is to be succinct but informative and enthusiastic. Don't try to make a sale at this point, but (if possible) do mention how you can add value to your new connection. Maybe the other person has no need for the tennis racquets you manufacture, but you can suggest really great restaurants for the trip they're taking. Always be able to offer something to the other person that will make them glad they took the time to talk to you.

Sometimes the best thing you can offer is conversation. This gives you the chance to bond over your shared experience and discover ways to help one another. For example: Can you provide insight into the keynote speaker's investment strategies? Are you able to introduce the other person to the groom's aunt because their children attend the same high school?

In my personal experience, I started a conversation with someone about cookies and months later placed him as a panelist for a noteworthy conference because he made an excellent and memorable impression on me. On more than one occasion, small talk has gotten me invited to networking events which led to unexpected opportunities such as job interviews, private parties, and more.

## Know When to Stop Pushing a Topic

Be prepared to change the subject if you hit a sore spot. Recognize subtle shifts in demeanor when you may be asking about a sensitive issue. Here is an example of a dialogue at a wedding reception that starts well but needs improvement:

**Ronit:** Your friend Peter just told me that your daughter loves riding horses. What sparked her interest in equestrian sports?

**Susan:** My daughter started riding at school when she was very young. I think they are starting to serve dinner. Are you getting steak or fish?

**Ronit:** How old was she? Does she prefer a certain type of horse? Would she be interested in learning to train them?

**Susan:** I'm going to get a cocktail. Have a nice day.

**Ronit:** But I haven't even gotten to know you!

In this scenario, Ronit was prepared with a conversation starter for engaging Susan. He took information he learned from Susan's friend Peter to ask about Susan's daughter. By mentioning Peter, Ronit was bringing credibility to his source. By asking about Susan's daughter, Ronit was appealing to Susan's attachment to her family. Ronit was leveraging to establish an immediate connection of trust and affection.

However, Susan is not fond of speaking about her daughter's passion for horseback riding, especially with strangers, because of a serious accident years prior. She tried to change the subject quickly, but Ronit didn't pick up her cue and bombarded her with further questions about the topic. Had Ronit noticed the change in Susan's demeanor and dropped the issue, he may have had a chance to salvage the conversation and build a rapport. Instead, he lost that opportunity by blindly pushing on a sore spot.

# Initiate

Obviously, you can't start every conversation already knowing which topics must be avoided for very individual reasons. A safe topic for one person, like international travel, might be a disaster with another person because of a crippling fear of flying. Close friends might forgive you, but complete strangers may simply stop talking to you mid-discussion.

Nonetheless, here are a list of 10 conversations you might try:

1. **"How did you find out about this event?"** You may discover that you go to the same gym, supermarket, or library.

2. **"How do you know the host?"** You'll find out more about the host. Maybe they're in the same Facebook group, they met at a juggling club, or they're relatives.

3. **"What was your favorite part of the keynote?"** Here's an opportunity to discuss a shared experience.

4. **"How would you improve the presentation we just saw?"** This gives you insight into what the other person values. Did they wish the speaker told emotional stories? Were they underwhelmed by the data charts? Will they be looking for further information?

5. **"What was the last movie you saw?"** Exchange opinions on the same movie or ask what they liked about the movie.

6. **"Which word best describes you?"** Use that word to formulate follow-up questions.

7. **"What are the most used apps on your phone?"** You'll learn how the other person allots their time and maybe find something useful for your life, too.

8. **"When did you last feel extremely challenged?"** This question will open the dialogue to discussing how the person overcomes obstacles.

9. **"How do you spend your free time?"** If you have overlapping interests, like golf or gardening, perhaps you can enjoy them together.

10. **"Who has had the most impact on your life?"** Most people enjoy talking about positive influences in their lives, and maybe you'll be invited to meet the person mentioned.

# Know How to Introduce Yourself

Any good conversation begins with good introductions. You should be prepared to introduce yourself in different situations and adapt to the environment. What you say to a new neighbor will be different from what you say to a new supervisor.

At the local grocery store, you might initiate a conversation about the neighborhood with a fellow customer. You can offer opinions to be discussed: "Did you see the cute coffee shop they're building next to the Apple Store? The gnome mural is adorable. I've had a fondness for gnomes since high school in Germany." Here, you've established that you're neighbors, and that you keep abreast of new developments in your shared city or town. You've given them your opinion about gnomes to agree or disagree about. Or if they have no opinions about gnomes, they can ask about your experiences in Germany.

Unless I'm in a professional setting, I like to start my chats with strangers in a very light and casual tone. People aren't usually looking for my thoughts on classical Greek philosophy when they're at the ice cream store with their three children.

At industry events, my introductions are much more precise because time is limited and everyone is focused on very specific goals. It is extremely important to catch people's attention as soon as possible because they are on a mission. After you provide your name, you might want a short transition before you slide in how you solve problems. "Hi. I'm Steve Wells and I think you were sitting two rows in front me during the 2:00 pm presentation in the Grand Ballroom. I've been a director at Microsoft for 20 years and I can tell you that the speaker's data is way outdated. Do you also work in machine learning?"

## Gracefully Enter a Group Conversation

Sometimes, you may want to join a group discussion that's already in progress. I will often stand near the cluster and listen in for topics and general tone of the conversation so I can sync up more easily. While I'm there, for no more than 20 seconds, I try to make eye contact and smile at a few people to make my presence known and hope that someone will invite me to join. If the circle widens to let me in, I will introduce myself if there's been a natural pause in the conversation. Otherwise, I prefer to remain silent and listen until I can insert myself gracefully. Aside from your introduction, it's best to refer to something that's already been said so people know you want to constructively comment.

What you don't want to do is force yourself into groups that are not relevant to you. What would you have to contribute to a gathering of sorority alumnae from a college you didn't attend? Why would you have any insight into a stranger's family drama about a pregnant teenager? Don't push your way into conversations where you can't add value or that have no relevance to your life. There are much better ways to spend your time. Avoid making the situation awkward for everyone.

# Establish Rapport

Successful small talk will establish rapport—that is, you'll feel a connection and familiarity with another person. The feeling of being strangers will dissipate in favor of mutual understanding and empathy.

The best way to build rapport is to show up with a friendly and positive attitude. Be happy that the other person is offering their time to get to know you better. Show your appreciation with a smile and greet them as if you're old friends already. Let the conversation flow. It's counterproductive to force this process along too quickly, and doing so may completely derail your goals.

The most valuable asset you have is your attention. Let the other person feel as though they have your full attention and that they are being heard. Show real interest in what is being said because it will help deepen any connections along the way. Ask thoughtful questions based on the comments they have made and occasionally repeat back what they've said by paraphrasing.

It's also nice to give genuine compliments. If you notice that they put care into a particular aspect of their life, show that you notice and ask more about it because people love talking about what brings them joy. Does your co-worker bring elaborate cakes to the office to share once a month? Praise them on their attention to detail and design. Do your in-laws spend every weekend working on their car collection? Tell them you're impressed by their skills in the garage.

# Find Common Ground

Another good tactic for building rapport is finding common ground. If you're in another person's space, such as their home or office, take inventory of the surroundings. Show interest in their interests. Is their home decorated with a nautical theme? Ask about the sailing trophy in the living room. Tell them about your fond memories of taking boat rides in Amsterdam.

Are you in a restaurant with a board game theme? Start a conversation to find the games you both enjoy and invite the other person to play with you. Try to keep the conversation and play casual while you find out more about the other person. If you're playing Scrabble, you can use the words as jumping points for new topics. "Triple letter score on the letter 'z' in 'blitz'! Kudos to you! Did you ever play football in college?"

The sports discussion can lead to finding out that you and the other person attended the same school. There's an automatic connection among alumni reminiscing about happy times as students even if there isn't a huge overlap. You may remember going to the local pizza place in town for weekly lunches with the marching band while the other person would go after monthly sorority meetings. However, you both remember the very quirky owner who always wore sequined cowboy hats with matching boots.

# Be a Little Vulnerable

Being a little vulnerable can also help develop trust and create engagement. While you're discussing stories from college, you might share an endearing tale from your sophomore year when you tried to serenade your girlfriend for your third anniversary but forgot the words to the song. You were utterly embarrassed at the time, but now you can laugh about the snafu with your new friend because you feel safe that you won't be shamed for it.

By showing that you're human and emotionally available, you open up the conversation to a deeper connection. You allow the other person to feel compassionate and less afraid to show their own vulnerabilities.

> By showing that you're human and emotionally available, you open up the conversation to a deeper connection.

Be careful not to overshare, however. You must be mindful of boundaries so you don't offer private details from your life that would make others cringe or feel uncomfortable. While you're trying to bond with the other person, it's important not to cross the line into inappropriate territory. Your son's new piano tutor shouldn't be hearing how your cousin's marriage problems are affecting the extended family.

Don't use vulnerability to fast-track relationships because you may end up alienating yourself. Misguided attempts to gain sympathy and build intimacy by oversharing personal matters will scare off the people you are trying to add to your life.

### Strangers are Not Instant Best Friends

Here is an example where a person's over-confidence causes the conversation they've started with a stranger to go quickly awry:

Saanvi: I cannot wait until the waitress comes back with my coffee.

Stranger: I love this cafe. They serve the best chai and almond croissants. What did you order?

Saanvi: I always start my morning off with a latte and chocolate glazed donut. I'm a total wreck otherwise.

Stranger: Oh, I hear you. I need that caffeine and sugar rush to get me going.

Saanvi: Right? Just last week, I was so coffee deprived that I wore two different shoes to the office.

Stranger: That's hilarious. Yesterday, I forgot my sneakers on the top of my car and drove off with them still on the sunroof! Here comes our food.

**Saanvi:** My ex-husband was like that. Very forgetful. He often forgot our daughter in the car when he was out running errands. It's not like he enjoyed being a father, though. In fact, he hated it. I finally divorced him when he almost killed my daughter during a camping trip. I never should have married him the first place.

**Stranger:** I'm so sorry . . . I need to run. There's a meeting at the office I forgot about.

Too much, too soon. Saanvi should have kept the conversation light and casual when the food arrived. Her oversharing scared off the stranger immediately. Her life story was way too intimate to confide in someone she had just met.

# Avoid Overused Lines and Topics

"The weather is so nice today. I love feeling the sun on my face."

I don't know when, but a long time ago, people decided to start a lot of small talk by discussing the weather. It's an easy and safe topic, but it's boring. My heart sinks when I hear it. "Here we go again . . . "

The greeting I like even less is, "How are you?" Most people will respond, "I'm fine, how are you?" without even thinking. "I'm fine" is the socially accepted and expected answer. This greeting is almost never intended to go anywhere. It additionally irks me because I feel like I'm lying when I'm really not fine. Sometimes, I really want to tell the person that I've had a terrible day that has mentally drained me. But that would be inappropriate, so I say, "I'm fine," before changing the subject quickly.

I would advise avoiding either of these conversation starters because they can potentially turn people off from continuing to speak with you. Try instead to start a discussion about your immediate surroundings or a shared experience you just had. "I love riding this elevator. It reminds me of all the weekend brunches my grandfather hosted for the family in the rooftop restaurant. And the art deco mirrors inspired me to become an art professor."

# Don't Be Too Eager

Be careful about looking overeager to make a connection. As discussed earlier, you definitely should not overshare in a bid to speed up a bond with someone you just met. Keep early conversations with strangers light and casual. Similarly, don't ask too many questions all at once. Doing so puts an undue burden on the other person and they will feel as if they are being interrogated. Always try to keep a good balance between your interest and being interesting. Don't make the person feel like they need to impress you or keep you from being bored. You should have something attractive to contribute to the exchange as well.

Give the other person your full attention, but don't be so intense as to come off creepy. Remember, you want the person to want to spend more time with you, not feel as if they're speaking to their stalker. You shouldn't mimic their every movement, agree with everything they say, and laugh heartily at every joke. No conversation should look remotely like this:

> "You're an iPhone user? So am I! We have so much in common! I don't even understand why anyone would ever be an Android user, am I right?"

> "You are the most brilliant person I've ever met! That is the funniest thing I've ever heard!"

> "We are soulmates. You are officially my best friend forever!"

# Use Humor and Have Fun

Using humor to bond is a wonderful tactic, because who doesn't like to laugh? Used appropriately, humor can ease tension and facilitate conversation. Dad jokes are great for this because they are purposely silly yet safe to utter, even in the presence of children. For example, let's say your teenage nephew spends all day cooking for his boyfriend and accidentally drops an entire lasagna all over your kitchen floor. After everyone stares for a second or two with their jaws dropped, you could break the silence by saying, "Cheer up, lad. It could be worse, you know. You could be stuck underground in a hole full of water. C'mon, you know I mean *well*."

Making people laugh diffuses awkward situations and makes a positive impact on the brain. Humor increases likeability, and when people like you, they're more likely to go along with what you want to do. Maybe you are trying to convince your teacher to give the class an extension on the final paper, or you want to close an international account with an important client. Humor is universal and an incredibly important tool that makes what you say more memorable than a booklet of boring statistics.

Some will use self-deprecating humor in attempts to build rapport. They'll tell embarrassing stories to present themselves as more relatable. Be careful in this practice because it can unintentionally make you look incompetent, which can be very difficult to rebound from. Try to use self-deprecating humor only if your audience already feels confident in their perception of you and your skills.

Landmine humor to avoid at all costs includes anything political, ethnic, racist, or sexist. Just don't. It's not worth the risk.

# Make a Game Out of It

Small talk doesn't have to be completely dreadful. Try making a game out of it. Maybe you'll wear an interesting pin on your outfit for a month and see how many people comment on it. Wear a different pin each month for a year and observe which pins receive the most feedback. Even though I meet a lot of new people on a fairly high frequency, I still like wearing something that catches the eye because it is such an easy avenue for someone to start a conversation with me. I'll sport bright green shoes, wear elaborate jewelry, or carry intricately designed bags. I'm also happy to use corporate-branded swag. People might just talk to me if they think I write for the *Wall Street Journal*.

If you're uncomfortable wearing anything that will catch attention, try to gamify your strategy. Try talking to at least three people at a networking event. Learn two facts about one new person once a month. See if guests at a holiday party are more open to discussing the caterer's melting ice sculpture or the host's library of books on beekeeping. Shape your experiences in ways that will compel you to continue your efforts and improve them. No one likes doing things that are soul-crushing, and small talk doesn't have to suck the life out of you. It can be fun!

### Don't Share Inappropriately (and Don't Be Creepy)

Haniya: I ride this bike path every weekend. I've never noticed that gazebo before. Do you know how long it's been there?

Stranger: They just put it in the park mid-week. I heard they're adding two outdoor ping-pong tables tomorrow.

Haniya: Fun! Do you play? I haven't played since college, but that was without paddles and with a lot of beer. Oh, good times! I used to get so incredibly drunk all the time. I maybe made it to half my classes sober. Now, as an adult, I go to the office sober half the time. Maybe less! Haha! Only twice have I stumbled into the fountain in the lobby. Okay . . . three times. But the third time doesn't really count because I didn't see the stupid new plant they put right next to the fountain! Who thought that would be a good idea? But enough about me, do you have children? I'd love to find another mother so we can coordinate play dates. Do you live in the area? You should come to my house for dinner!

This conversation would scare me away immediately, even if I didn't have children or live in the area. Haniya is trying too hard to be perceived as fun, and so she just comes off as an irresponsible alcoholic. Her questions about children and where the other person lives are also premature. Inviting a stranger to her house for dinner after two sentences is an extremely poor attempt at forcing a quick bond. Haniya looks desperate and unstable to say the least.

## Remember This

- Take the task seriously, but have fun with it whenever appropriate. Meeting new people will be less of a chore if you look forward to the experience.

- Don't be too eager. Reeking of desperation will make you seem like a stalker. Coming off as creepy will be counterproductive.

- Show that you appreciate the time others are willing to give you. Make them feel heard and valued for their conversation.

## CHAPTER FOUR

# LISTEN ACTIVELY

Active listening is essential for developing strong rapport and eventually deeper bonds because your engagement with others becomes more empathetic. Truly hearing what someone is saying informs your future interactions with them since you understand their point of view. You're listening with intent. You're not solely focused on your own agenda, what you think you hear, or what you want to hear.

Developing and practicing active listening skills is important in making you a better communicator and problem-solver. When someone is speaking, it's just as critical to absorb what is being said beyond the literal words coming out of their mouths.

# Let the Other Person Talk

Maintaining a balanced ratio of talking time between each person is important because it lets everyone feel like they've been given time to be heard. Even if you don't agree with a person, give them the space to speak and expand on their comments. Not only is it respectful, it will give you greater insight into their thoughts.

Understanding each other's perspectives means being able to more effectively work on solutions. If you don't know the other person's point of view, how can you begin to help them? If you're dominating the conversation, you're not giving the other person any time to voice their concerns.

> Understanding each other's perspectives means being able to more effectively work on solutions. If you don't know the other person's point of view, how can you begin to help them?

Letting the other person speak makes them feel that their opinions are valued. It signals to them that you care.

Imagine you're the new parent of twins. Suddenly you need a new affordable vehicle for your expanded family. You've gone to the dealership to look for a minivan to fit everyone comfortably but the salesperson keeps insisting you look at expensive little sports cars. You probably don't feel that your salesperson cares about you or that you've been heard at all. The salesperson has an agenda they are forcing on you for their own interests.

In contrast, imagine you're at a second car dealership. Not only does the second salesperson show you a variety of minivans that match your preferences, they cheerfully explain child-friendly new features and help you finance your purchase at a lower price point than you had budgeted. You would give that second salesperson your business because you felt heard and valued as a customer.

# Listen for Meaning Beyond the Words

Trisha had another long night at the office. For the past two months, there had not been a single weeknight that she made it home in time to have dinner with her husband, Darnell. Even in bed, she worked late into the night, determined to get a promotion at the law firm by the end of the year. Her extended hours were putting a strain on her marriage. She and Darnell had been arguing constantly since her workload increased. He would often complain about eating supper alone, and she just cut him short. "What is the big deal about dining alone? This promotion is way more important than any mushroom ravioli! Why can't you be supportive of me? I'm doing this for both of us!"

Every conversation ended up in a heated screaming match or tears of frustration. While Darnell did not like eating alone, his deeper distress was actually a fear of being left behind personally and professionally. His career was stagnant while she was a rising star. Trisha allowed herself to become so tunnel-visioned that she could not empathize with the sense of abandonment Darnell was feeling. Her defensiveness about her ambitions made her stubbornly demand that he provide emotional support without asking for any in return. Without active listening, their marriage would be doomed.

Trisha and Darnell needed to listen to each other without being defensive. They should each have said, "What do you really need from me? I will try to offer you what you need. Also, this is what I need from you."

# Use Short Verbal Affirmations

Short verbal affirmations are simple words, phrases, and sounds that help indicate that you're listening and convey understanding. Even though these are small words or short phrases, they can have a meaningful impact. Some examples include:

- Yes

- Okay

- Hmm

- Right

- Really

- Indeed

- Definitely

- I understand

- I see your point of view

- That's understandable

# Don't Mentally Prepare Your Responses

It's very easy to let yourself become distracted by preparing your response. You may be eager to reply to show off your knowledge, impatient to make a sale, or worried you'll forget what you planned on saying. Mentally putting together a response while the other person is still speaking can backfire because they can tell by your eyes and general expression that you are not fully and actively listening. They feel that they don't have your full attention and that, because of this, they won't get a response based on everything they've just tried to convey to you.

Try not to overthink your engagement and stay focused on the person speaking. Don't let your mind wander. Here are some tips:

- Hide your phone where it cannot distract you with blinking or vibrating alerts.

- Maintain proper eye contact with the other person; don't look around the room.

- Nod your head while you're listening to affirm that you're paying attention.

Put your entire focus on what is being said instead of what you will say in response. Try to understand why the other person feels the way they do and why certain details are important to them. Being fully present will show that you care.

## Don't Assume

It's also very easy to make assumptions about what another person is saying because our minds like to race to conclusions. Worse, we might voice those automatic conclusions in an attempt to hasten rapport by showing that we were listening and completely understand. If we are wrong or misguided, however, the situation is ripe for tension. It's proof that we were not actively listening and not as empathetic as we ought to be.

The danger in making assumptions is that the conclusions our mind comes up with are always colored by our own experiences and biases, neither of which will be exactly those of the person speaking. So, you'll never completely understand what someone else is going through. Experts warn against saying, "I know exactly how you feel." You don't.

The most welcome contribution you can bring to a conversation is active listening without judgment or assumptions. Let the person talk and tell you how they feel or tell you what actually happened, because you don't know. Don't guess.

> The most welcome contribution you can bring to a conversation is active listening without judgment or assumptions.

You can lessen the risk of embarrassing or upsetting assumptions by patiently listening without interruption. Don't make the situation about you or how you feel. Don't cut the other person off with your own similar story.

# Paraphrase to Demonstrate Understanding

A great strategy to demonstrate that you've been listening and to avoid making assumptions is to paraphrase what you've just been told into a question. This way, you can confirm that you understand correctly, and it gives you an easy opportunity to ask further questions. For example:

**Friend:** Imani thinks working for a big tech company like Google or Microsoft will greatly improve her resume.

**You:** It sounds like you're saying that she is thinking about moving to the West Coast for better career opportunities. Am I understanding correctly?

Paraphrasing to demonstrate understanding is particularly useful for clarifying what has been said and what you heard. It helps bridge the gap of comprehension sometimes inherent in language. No one can anticipate every detail that the other person needs to hear or know how the other person will connect the dots between the pieces of information they received. This is why people have discussions, and the most effective discussions are those where people listen actively, ask for clarification, and confirm understanding.

## Listen Before You Get Defensive

Using the techniques discussed in this chapter can really help improve relationships. For example, it helped Zainab and Jenna bring harmony back to their relationship as roommates.

**Zainab:** I know you think I'm a nag, but can you please not leave your stuff all over our living room all the time? It's appalling.

**Jenna:** For the record, I don't think you're a nag. I miss when we used to spend lots of time together. We used to laugh so much.

**Zainab:** What happened to us?

**Jenna:** Work got busy for both of us. More for you than me, and I've really missed you these past months.

**Zainab:** Look, I'm going to clear my schedule so we have the whole weekend together, okay?

**Jenna:** Yes, please. And I'll clean up the living room by Friday.

You can see in Zainab and Jenna's conversation how making assumptions and being defensive can wreak havoc. Only when both were willing to actively listen and clarify what the other person felt were they able to reach a happy solution to satisfy everyone.

# Remember This

- Don't make assumptions. Rather, paraphrase for clarity.

- Listen actively and fully to what the other person is saying, not just to what you want to hear.

- Try to empathize with the other person and understand their perspective, history, and experiences.

## CHAPTER FIVE
# PRACTICE KINDNESS

One of the best strategies for bringing positivity to every conversation is by practicing kindness. When you are kind, the gesture boosts your emotional well-being as well as the recipient's. It's a win-win.

In fact, if you make kindness an automatic daily routine, it will promote longevity by increasing your overall happiness while decreasing feelings of loneliness. Small but regular acts of kindness, like offering a genuine compliment, cost nothing but can make a big impact.

Think about the last time you had a really bad day and someone took the time to be kind to you. That moment probably restored your faith in humanity and immediately improved your mood. Try doing that for someone else every day. You'll be happier for it.

# Offer Appropriate Compliments

Offering appropriate compliments is an easy way to practice kindness and is an important skill to be developed. Like any other talent, practice will improve your delivery and comfort level. Some specific compliments you might offer someone include:

- You are so much fun to be around!

- I really appreciate your sense of humor.

- Your question after this morning's keynote was fantastic.

- I deeply admire your courage.

- Your speech to the students was truly inspiring.

- I find your perspective refreshing.

- Your sense of adventure is awesome.

- I admire your grit; not everyone can do what you've done.

Try to compliment people on their accomplishments. Make them feel recognized for the work they've put into achieving their goals. Acknowledge them for the effort they've invested in the journey they've chosen.

The key is sincerity plus positivity. You should always avoid compliments that may be well-intentioned but are actually patronizing, triggering, or rude.

It's also safer to stay clear of complimenting someone on their physical appearance. Plus, it's just more meaningful to compliment someone on their achievements. Would you rather hear that you have pretty eyes or that someone thinks your book deserves a Pulitzer Prize? Put yourself in the other person's position. What would they want to be complimented on for accomplishing?

# Microaggressions

Years ago, I was on a first date with a Caucasian man. After about 10 minutes of conversation, he said to me, "Your English is very good." I furrowed my brow and asked, "Why wouldn't it be? I was born and raised here in New York City." Today, I can even add, "In fact, I graduated from a master's program at an Ivy League school with a creative writing thesis, I have been published in *Forbes* multiple times, and I wrote a 200-page book in less than a year."

It's not uncommon for Asian Americans to be told, "You speak English really well." It's a microaggression, which *Harvard Business Review* defines as "incidents in which someone accidentally (or purposely) makes an offensive statement or asks an insensitive question. Microaggressions are defined as verbal, behavioral, and environmental indignities that communicate hostile, derogatory, or negative racial slights and insults to the target person or group."

Several more examples of microaggressions include:

"For being Black, you get along really well with white people."

"You're so pretty, I didn't think you'd be a lesbian."

"I'm jealous you got into college on affirmative action."

Some people will offer these comments as compliments, while others are more malicious in their intent. Either way, these statements are microaggressions to avoid because they are deleterious to relationship building. Be mindful of your privileges so you don't hurt others by making them feel their exclusion and discrimination from dominant groups. Don't amplify stereotypes.

# Gracefully Accept Compliments

Just as it's a skill to give compliments, it's a skill to gracefully accept compliments. Learning to do so will keep the situation from becoming awkward. In order to avoid coming across as a conceited jerk, most people will downplay, deflect, dilute, or reject compliments immediately. These are not the best tactics because they make the person giving the compliment feel rejected. It's much better to train yourself to accept kind words with grace and humility. For example, here are two responses you may use with a friendly tone and smile:

- I appreciate the compliment, thank you so much.

- Thank you, it's kind of you to say.

If you are being complimented on a team project, share the credit. Recognize the contributions your colleagues made toward the shared success. Many leaders like to say something along the lines of:

- I could not have done it without the help of my team.

- I could not have gotten here alone. My entire team deserves a big round of applause.

Avoid undermining the compliments you receive with comments such as, "It was no big deal," or, "Anyone could have done the same." Respect that the person speaking with you is recognizing your work. You should also stay clear of compliment competitions, especially with those you admire. This is not the time to downplay your own achievements in contrast to theirs. Simply let the other person compliment you fully before you thank them sincerely.

## Kindness Works Both Ways

Part of being kind is gracefully allowing others to be kind to you. Learn to allow others to compliment you. If you cannot, this may become an obstacle for connecting to others, as Arham found out while volunteering for a fundraiser:

**Amanda:** I love your banner design. It's so creative! I would never have thought of having the turtle as the focal point.

**Arham:** Oh, anyone could have thought of it. It's nothing special.

**Amanda:** You're too humble. All the kids loved it, too. They're still taking selfies with it!

**Arham:** They're just kids. It's really no big deal.

**Amanda:** Well, okay. Enjoy the rest of the event. I'm going to refresh my drink.

Instead of graciously acknowledging the good job he had done designing the banner, he downplayed his talents because he didn't want to seem conceited. However, his decision to appear humble made Amanda feel personally rejected. To her, his replies sounded as if her opinions didn't matter much. Even when she tried a second time to compliment him, he deflected. Arham's comments effectively destroyed any potential rapport in that moment—so much so that Amanda walked away.

# Use Compliments as a Jumping Off Point

Compliments are a great way to keep the conversation going. You can use compliments as a launchpad for other topics you would like to discuss. For example, you start a great discussion about 90s music after the DJ plays a Backstreet Boys song that you both loved during high school. This turns into a hilarious debate about other boy bands such as N*SYNC and 98 Degrees. While you're feeling more comfortable with each other, you might subtly steer the conversation toward fashion of that decade, then how you admire the other person's sense of style. You can really lock in that feel-good moment with a compliment about how they have an eye for design. Knowing that fashion is something that matters to the other person will compel them to continue speaking with you about their interest. Maybe they'll even offer you opportunities you didn't expect.

Being acknowledged for something meaningful makes people want to talk more and reciprocate the kindness. I give career talks and workshops on a regular basis. I always love when people make an effort to thank me after my presentations. They tell me that my advice is useful and practical. It makes me feel great, and it leaves a positive impression on my mind. I've made lovely friendships this way and voluntarily helped others in their professional careers as a result.

# Ask for and Offer Favors and Resources

Many people ask me for favors after they see my resources and connections. This works when I am asked in a tactful way that makes me feel good and kind about helping another person. This does not work when the person makes demands of me out of sheer entitlement.

Both asking for and offering favors should be done in tactful and appropriate ways that enhance a relationship. I love being able to offer favors because the gesture is a positive contribution to an interaction.

However, asking for favors has never been a strength of mine because it makes me feel indebted to another person. It's a mindset I need to break, because studies have shown that appropriately asking for favors makes you seem more likeable! This makes sense if you think about it. The other person is giving you the opportunity to do something that makes you feel good.

> "Sure, I'll help you move the chairs to the other side of the room."

> "Yes, I'll teach you how to paint."

> "No problem, I'll watch your dog for 10 minutes."

Out of necessity, I once forced myself to ask a complete stranger to take my photo on a rooftop hotel. We remain friends to this day because of that simple request. Maybe it was the Benjamin Franklin effect, where your brain thinks, "Well, I did that favor for this person, so it must be because I like that person. Obviously, I wouldn't do a favor for someone I don't like!"

### Be Conversational, Not Transactional

**Scenario A:**

Many people go to networking events because they are looking for jobs. Too many neglect to form a relationship before asking for a favor. Note the difference between Rosa and Canberk's strategies with Lauren:

**Rosa:** My dream is to work at Google in cybersecurity. Can you help me get a job there?

**Lauren:** The interview process is very rigorous. What are your qualifications?

**Rosa:** My background is in real estate, but I'm sure I can learn cybersecurity quickly. I just need you to put me in

→

touch with the hiring manager in cybersecurity. What's their name and email?

**Scenario B:**

Canberk: Your presentation was incredibly informative. It provided me with a better sense of the culture at Google.

Lauren: Thank you, my team spent a lot of working on this event tonight.

Canberk: I'm really interested in learning more about the company and exploring a fit with my background. Given our mutual interest in public healthcare, I would appreciate the chance to show you a mobile app I've been working on for the past year.

Lauren: Let me take your contact information, and we can set up an informational meeting for next week. I'd love to help you if I can or point you in the direction you need.

Canberk: Thank you so much!

Rosa's approach was much too transactional and entitled. She didn't try to build any rapport with Lauren, and simply demanded information. If she's remembered for anything, it will be her rudeness.

In contrast, Canberk began his conversation with Lauren with a compliment that showed he valued the work that her team put into the presentation. He actively listened to her talk and appealed to their mutual interest in public healthcare. His tone was humble, and he expressed appreciation that Lauren would consider looking at his work. Lauren was unsurprisingly more open to continuing the conversation with Canberk and helping him in some capacity.

# Don't Complain

The room is too hot. The room is too small. There was too much traffic on the way over. The food is terrible and the service is slow. There is no end to the things we can complain about. And we do. It's easy to complain, and sometimes it's the easiest way to bond with someone. If we dislike something, we want others to dislike it, too. In very, very small doses, this can be acceptable. However, don't rely on complaining as a go-to bonding experience.

If you are always finding something to complain about, you will be marked as the complainer. You do not want that. Think about it. Would you gravitate toward someone who is always complaining? It's mentally exhausting and not fun. Instead, be more self-aware and put more positivity into your encounters. Eliminate negative statements.

While griping may be natural, we can make a habit of working toward more uplifting thinking. Any time you catch yourself saying something negative, turn it into a positive. For example, "The room is too hot, so it gave me a good reason to step into the garden and admire the flowers and water fountain." Or, "There was too much traffic on the way over, but it gave me time to come up with a really great toast for the newlyweds."

There will always be things to complain about. Don't just complain about them; find solutions to eliminate them. You'll feel better about life and people will respect you more.

# Be Careful with Criticism

One of the worst things you can do is trash talk about someone, be it a mutual friend, an ex-lover, a superior, or a stranger. It may be tempting, but it's a dangerous pitfall that you may not be able to recover from once the damage is done. There are so many levels to this risk:

**It's unpleasant.** It's tiresome to be around people who are always harping on others. This kind of behavior is highly unpleasant and will drive others away from you.

**It erodes trust.** If you are a gossip, how do others know that you won't turn around and spread rumors about them? Instead, be purposeful in your positivity and uplift others even if they don't know about it.

**It jeopardizes your connections.** Let's go back to the scenario with Rosa and Canberk. Suppose Rosa tells Canberk that she thinks Lauren is rude, incompetent, and unhelpful. There's no reason for him to believe this is true based on his own interaction with Lauren, so he may guess that Rosa was being antagonizing in their exchange. He's not going to undermine his own chances by even being seen speaking with Rosa anymore, so he leaves the conversation as soon as possible. You can see how this would play out for Rosa across many other scenarios, repeatedly.

### No One Likes a Negative Nancy

In general, just remember to be kind, genuine, and uplifting in your conversations. Nagaco doesn't live the perfect life, but she always tries to be upbeat and it has helped her sustain great friendships over the years.

**Nagaco:** That reminds me, how is your keynote on negotiations going?

**Carlos:** I'm just finishing up the conclusion. That's always the most difficult section for me.

**Nagaco:** I'm sure it will be great.

**Carlos:** Well, it can't be any worse than Julia's presentation on blockchain and cryptocurrency.

**Nagaco:** Be nice. You know she worked hard on that. She just needs to learn to pace herself better.

**Carlos:** You are always so compassionate.

**Nagaco:** Thank you. The world needs more compassion in it, and I try to do my part. My son and I were scheduled to volunteer at the church soup kitchen next weekend, but we had to cancel because our car is still at the repair shop.

**Carlos:** I'm free next week, why don't I drive you to and from the church so you and your son can volunteer?

**Nagaco:** We'd be so grateful!

**Carlos:** Just doing my part, with you as my example.

# Remember This

- Be genuine, specific, and succinct about your compliments. Recognize others for their accomplishments.

- Make a habit of being positive and showing kindness on a daily basis. It will improve your mental well-being, as well as the well-being of those around you.

- Don't just complain about problems; work towards finding solutions for them. Give people reasons to gravitate toward you instead of away from you.

# CHAPTER SIX
# DEEPEN THE CONVERSATION

Once you've had a bit of conversation, there's an opportunity to engage in more meaningful ways. Small talk should be the gateway to connect with another person more deeply and walk away having learned something new. There's little point to limiting all of your conversations to the weather and food. People naturally crave more—to give more and to get more.

Conversations should be invigorating and captivate your attention. If you can deepen your conversation with someone, you also deepen your connection with them. This is when you start building rapport and developing trust. With trust, a relationship will naturally form.

# Read Your Listener

Being able to read your listener is an important skill for successful communication. If you can tell what you're saying is not reaching your audience, it's time to pivot.

Here are five signals that people are starting to tune out or get bored:

1. They're not maintaining eye contact. Their eyes are wandering around the room as you speak.

2. They're checking their phone every time a new notification or alert pops up.

3. They're checking their watch to see how much longer they have to pretend they are listening.

4. Their body language is restless, like they need to escape. They fidget a lot.

5. Their conversation is stilted. They answer your questions with one or two words.

If you notice any of these behaviors, it's time to alter the course of your conversation if you want it to continue. Maybe change the subject so they change their interest in speaking with you.

Here are five signals that people are engaged and ready to talk more:

1. You have their full attention. They're maintaining eye contact and smiling.

2. They are not distracted by their phone. They never look at it during the conversation.

3. Their body points to yours. They are physically leaning in toward you.

4. They ask questions. They want more information from you.

5. They willingly offer more information about themselves, without being asked.

# Be Present

You can't expect other people to give you their full attention if you are not mentally present. You must be committed to your conversations. This means that you have cleared your mind of distractions to give the other person your entire focus and attention. You are not thinking about the past or the future. You are present and you are actively listening, as discussed in an earlier chapter.

If, instead, you are mentally elsewhere while talking to others, your thinking will automatically be narrower in perspective and your brain will take cognitive shortcuts. In the *Financial Post*, Ray William points to studies by neuroscientist and author Daniel Siegel that find that this behavior leads to "oversimplification, curtailed curiosity, reliance on ingrained beliefs and the perceptional blind spots . . . Mindfulness practices enable individuals to jettison judgment and develop more flexible reactions."

Basically, you'll be cheating yourself and the other person of a meaningful interaction if you aren't focused. Try slowing down so you can really be in the moment. Stop thinking about what you need to do next. Appreciate that being more mindful and self-aware will enhance your discussions because your brain will be less cluttered by other mental noise. You'll gain a clarity which will allow you to express yourself better and improve your decision-making.

## Talking to Teenagers

Parents commonly struggle with having meaningful conversations with their teenagers. It's especially difficult these days when everyone keeps busy schedules and has a mobile phone that relentlessly sends alerts and notifications. Find space in both of your schedules that lends itself to having a longer talk. Oftentimes, that will be at the dinner table, especially if you do not allow electronic devices to be accessed during meals so everyone is mentally present.

→

It's important to create a "safe space" atmosphere so everyone feels comfortable to be honest and vulnerable. Let others know they are invited to share what is going on in their lives, positive and negative. Don't jump to criticize or judge. Listen with compassion. The teenage years are a difficult time in many people's lives. If you don't show support early on, you risk closing off communication, which makes it harder to build trust long-term.

Be patient. Don't rush through the conversation with quick solutions. It's helpful to address concerns on a regular basis rather than reacting only when things hit a crisis point. Plus, if you steadily learn more about your children's lives with a daily frequency, you'll have a much better idea of how they think and respond to different circumstances.

# Express Curiosity

I'll be honest with you: If I was at an event and I saw someone in a hat and shirt branded with large NASCAR logos, they would not be the first person I'd consider approaching. What would we have to talk about? Obviously, they are a huge NASCAR fan, while I have never watched one race.

One should always keep an open mindset because you can learn something new with every conversation. Not everyone is going to have the same interests as you, and that should be a good thing. It means you can gain new knowledge. Plus, you never know where the conversation might end up.

While I might not know much about NASCAR, I can ask questions about it until I find an aspect about the sport that holds my attention. For example, the person might explain to me that American stock car racing originated during Prohibition when bootleg whiskey was distributed by drivers in fast, small cars modified for the task. After Prohibition was repealed in 1933, the races continued for profit and pride in the rural southern regions of the United States.

I might then use that moment to switch into talking about the Rolex Cosmograph Daytona, which was designed specifically for racing drivers. I'm not passionate about stock car racing, but I am about wristwatches. With some luck, we could find that we have a mutual interest in horology and become fast friends because of it.

# Steer the Conversation Where You Want It

Tactfully steering a discussion to a topic you want to talk about is a skill. Many people can be turned off by others who start conversations with a direct request. It feels overly transactional. There's no building of rapport, just an ask. This is where small talk comes in.

Suppose you know that your co-worker is a basketball fan. You could start a conversation asking if they followed the Boston Celtics and Los Angeles Lakers rivalry in the 1980s. You might recommend that they watch the ESPN documentary episode "Best of Enemies," which shows how the two competing teams saved the NBA. Maybe you even invite them to go to a game with you and have drinks afterwards.

After you establish mutual interests with the co-worker, it will be easier to steer the conversation where you want because you've developed a rapport and spent time together. It will be easier for them to envision working with you if your goal is to suggest joining a project they are leading.

People are much more open to working with those they like and share commonalities with. Working with strangers is fraught with risk. You don't know if your personalities are compatible, you don't know if the person is reliable, etc. Building a rapport beforehand makes the transition to a stronger relationship, like collaborating on a work project, much smoother.

## Rapport Paves the Way for Success

Based on the concepts discussed in this chapter, notice how differently these two conversations go:

**Scenario A:**

Jimin: I read that you landed the wellness client in Arizona.

Jill: Yes.

Jimin: I'd like to join your team in a finance role.

Jill: I already have someone in mind for that position.

Jimin: I really think we'd work well together.

Jill: I'm not sure what you're basing that assumption on. I'm sorry, I'm heading to a meeting.

**Scenario B:**

Jimin: So how did you become interested in basketball?

Jill: Growing up, my grandfather worked long hours to support the family. He worked seven days a week, and often past 9:00 pm. But he always spent an hour before dinner shooting hoops with me in the driveway. It was our ritual.

Jimin: He sounds like a good man.

Jill: He was a great man!

Jimin: I'll toast to that!

Jill: This one is for Pop-Pop!

Jimin: And a toast to you! I read that you landed the wellness client in Arizona. In fact, you beat three Fortune 100 teams for it.

Jill: I worked for three weeks on that proposal. Two hours before the presentation, I caught an error in the data.

Jimin: Yikes. Well, I'd be more than happy to join your team. They don't call me Mr. Eagle Eyes for nothing.

Jill: I can tell by the way you scrutinized the check after our dinner. Haha. Sure, let's set up a time to talk in the office tomorrow.

Jimin: Perfect. I previously worked with the data scientist on the client's team, and I can show you how they've used statistics for their experiments in the past.

Jill: I wish I had met you before two months ago!

Jimin: The feeling is mutual.

In the first conversation, Jimin didn't get any traction with Jill because there was no rapport established between them. Jimin just went in for the ask and Jill wasn't open to learning more because he was basically a stranger. He was an unknown entity.

In the second conversation, Jimin spent time getting to know Jill and let her get to know him through shared experiences. He genuinely complimented her grandfather and her success at landing an important client for the company. Given their time together, Jill discovered that

Jimin is detail-oriented, funny, and ambitious. They have mutual interests and compatible personalities. He also brings valuable experience to her project. Jimin was much more successful in reaching his goal in the second scenario because he invested the time to build a relationship with Jill before the ask.

# Ask About Them

Building rapport involves getting to know people by asking questions about them. In the early stages, you don't want to get overly personal because you should respect boundaries. It's too soon to have intimate conversations when you're still in the process of building up to a deeper connection. Here are some questions you might ask that can lead to more specific inquires later:

## Work

- What made you decide to join the company?

- Since joining the company, what is the biggest impact you've made?

- Where would you like to see the company go in the next five years?

## Family

- How long has your family lived in the area?

- Which family member do you feel the closest to and why?

- What is your favorite memory from family vacations?

## Interests

- When did you become interested in this area?

- What is the most surprising aspect of your interest?

- How much time do you dedicate to learning about this interest?

## Hobbies

- What kind of person is drawn to this hobby?

- Do you have any funny stories related to your hobby?

- Do you share this hobby with any family members?

Be careful not to use these suggestions simply as a list to run down in a conversation. Remember, you want the other person to learn about you also. There should be a balance in what both of you are learning about one another. You're not there to interrogate the other person about their life.

# Ask Open-Ended Questions

If you are speaking with someone and the conversation stalls, here are some go-to open ended questions that are widely applicable and useful at keeping the conversation going:

- What's been most memorable about your week so far?

- What are you looking forward to this month?

- Are you watching the new season of [the most popular TV series]? How do you like it?

- How are your projects progressing? Do you need help with anything?

- What other issues are important to you? What are your top priorities?

- What is the biggest problem you would like to see solved?

- I need to think about that more. Would you elaborate to help me understand better?

- What were your expectations for this event, and were your expectations met?

- What is the process you use to make decisions?

- Which opportunities do you find the most attractive and why?

Open-ended questions are valuable in continuing a conversation because they require responses beyond a simple "yes" or "no." They give you new information and insight to build a more robust discussion. Moreover, they signal to the other person that you're interested in learning more. Use these questions as a supplement to your active listening, not as a script. You may be pleasantly surprised by the outcomes.

# Ask Follow-up Questions

The key to asking good follow-up questions is active listening. If you listen with intention, you will be able to come up with questions that deepen the conversation and signal that you have been paying attention to what has been said. Read the speaker to get a sense of where they would like the discussion to go and adjust your questions accordingly. For example:

- Your daughter sounds like she's completely on top of the college admissions process. Which schools top her list and why?

- You're saying the team lead isn't delegating well. Is everyone's strength matched with the tasks they are assigned?

- Planning your niece's wedding has taken up so much of your time. A professional planner really helped me streamline the process. Would you like the name of the one I hired?

You don't want to go into conversations with a strict script that has no regard for what the other person is saying. You should be reacting, not just reciting a list of questions you prepared beforehand. Questions that seem like they're out of left field show that you have not been actively listening and you are not engaged.

# Expand on Details

When you're engaged in small talk, stories can have a powerful impact if they are delivered in a way that moves the person listening. Memorable stories captivate and engage. When you tell a story, expand on details so your audience easily understands and envisions what you are trying to convey.

Compare the following two versions of the same story:

**Version One:** I was really sick mid-March because I caught COVID-19. I slept a lot and had a fever. I eventually recovered without going to the hospital.

**Version Two:** I was suffering from coronavirus in mid-March, but I wasn't certain because the symptoms were similar to allergies and the flu. Tests weren't widely available at the time. After about a week of respiratory problems, my body needed a minimum of 13 hours of sleep a night for five consecutive days. I was so exhausted, I didn't have the energy to walk from the bedroom to the kitchen and back. I skipped meals because I was too tired to cook. I also lost my appetite. During the second week, I developed a fever of 101°F. Mentally, I was scared and sad because I had no one to look after me. I was convinced that I was going to die alone.

The second story is much more dramatic for the listener because it connects on an emotional level. There is a robustness missing from the first story. You "slept a lot" versus "my body needed a minimum of 13 hours of sleep a night for five consecutive days." "I eventually recovered" versus "I was scared and sad . . . I was going to die alone." The first story is simple and matter-of-fact while the second story draws in the listener with gripping descriptions.

# Match Their Mood

Just as matching a person's body language helps create a subconscious mental bond, matching the mood of the other person will foster a connection and keep the conversation going. Imagine one person is depressed and the other is laughing. That kind of disjointed exchange is awkward. Neither person will leave the moment feeling that the other person understood them.

Let's continue the coronavirus story from above as an example:

> **Li-San:** I had no one to look after me. I was convinced that I was going to die alone.

> **Sam:** You weren't going to die alone!

> **Li-San:** Why are you telling me what I know is not true?

> **Sam:** You have family. And friends.

> **Li-San:** My family would escalate the situation and make me even more upset. I refused to tell them. And my friends . . . I have no friends to rely on for this kind of situation.

> **Sam:** I always make sure my friends and family will be there when I need them. Like if I got COVID-19.

**Li-San:** Lucky you. I can't say the same.

**Sam:** When I had surgery on my legs, my college roommate even flew cross-country to visit. And he brought a dozen of my favorite bagels for me.

**Li-San:** I lost touch with everyone from school.

**Sam:** When I was discharged from the hospital, my father built me a ramp so it'd be easier for me to get in and out of my house.

Here, Sam shows absolutely no understanding of the situation. He's not reading Li-San's mood or matching it. First, he negates what Li-San has told him about dying alone. Then, he makes the conversation completely about himself. He's not reacting to what is being said. Finally, he outright boasts about his circumstances.

Li-San would understandably be upset by Sam's blatant disregard for her sadness. She needed empathy and received none. At the end of the conversation, she feels completely unfulfilled and even worse than when she started talking to Sam.

# Expand the Group

It often makes sense to bring more people into a conversation to be inclusive, to facilitate networking, or to offer new perspectives. A few tips for tactfully opening up the conversation to new people include:

**Making new people feel that their opinion makes a difference.**
The high school principal might nominate several sophomores to join a committee tasked with the redesign of the new technology lab for students. "We want to hear your thoughts during the renovation process because you will be the ones using the space. We want to avoid making decisions without your input. You have a say in what gets built."

**Enlisting new people for their expertise.** The senior vice president might task the interns with creating new marketing campaigns that primarily use social media popular with young teenagers. "You are digital natives who grew up using social media, so you know it in a way that I don't. I'm asking you to apply the knowledge you've collected to come up with ideas for advertising to the age group right under yours."

**Inviting new people to share their experiences.** The volunteer coordinator might choose individuals with relevant backgrounds to lead culture classes. "Since you lived most of your lives in the countries we're trying to serve, we'd like you to teach the rest of us about social norms. We want to be sensitive to cultural differences and avoid offending anyone."

Basically, anytime you would like to invite new people to a conversation, let them know why their contributions matter. Are they bringing a certain expertise, a great personality, more diversity, or something else? What value do they add to the discussion?

### Seamlessly Add New People to Conversations

Here are conversational examples that demonstrate how techniques discussed in this chapter can completely change the flow of a discussion:

**Jordan:** Hey Kami, come join us.

(No introduction of Kami to the group.)

**Pamela:** People are choosing smaller homes because they need less maintenance.

(Pamela doesn't acknowledge the new addition to the conversation.)

**Kami:** Did you guys watch the series finale of *The Office*? It was brilliant!

(Kami doesn't introduce himself. He plunges in without listening to the existing conversation and starts talking about something completely different.)

A less fragmented version of the same scenario is improved when everyone contributes to the quality of the conversation:

**Jordan:** Hey Kami, come join us. I want you to meet Pamela because you're both environmental activists. Pamela was just telling me how there's a trend of people downsizing.

(Jordan invites Kami to the group and introduces him to Pamela based on their mutual interest. He gives a quick statement about the topic being discussed so Kami knows what is going on.)

**Pamela:** Hi, Kami. It's nice to meet you. I was just explaining to Jordan that people are choosing smaller homes because they need less maintenance.

(Pamela welcomes Kami into the conversation and engages him immediately.)

**Kami:** I am really happy about the trend towards downsizing. As our society becomes less consumeristic, we'll do less damage to the environment. What is your opinion about the new law designed to curb our carbon footprint?

(Kami gives the discussion his full attention and responds to what Pamela said with positivity. He asks for her thoughts in a relevant follow-up question to show interest in continuing to talk about the topic.)

# Remember This

- Read your listener and match the mood. If you don't do so, you risk losing their attention or creating a very uncomfortable situation.

- Deepen the conversation by expressing your curiosity and asking meaningful follow-up questions based on what you are hearing. Navigate the conversation in a way that makes it flow naturally. Don't rely on a script of what you plan to say.

- Incorporate stories that are memorable, captivating, and engaging. Use details to connect emotionally and build rapport.

## CHAPTER SEVEN

# RECOVER SMOOTHLY

It's impossible for anyone to have a perfect conversation every time they speak with someone else. It's common for conversations to become awkward, boring, or uncomfortable. Sometimes, conversations will even turn inappropriate.

Being able to smooth out rough conversations is an incredibly useful skill. Saving a conversation that's gone wrong can even help with making a lasting positive impression. The key is bringing the discussion back into focus, steering it back in the right direction.

Think back to an earlier point where you and the other person were aligned in mood, and reference that moment. For example, "I just remembered that I wanted to ask you about the trip you took last year. Would you recommend any hotels within walking distance of the opera house you mentioned?"

# Overcome Awkward Silence

Conversations will sometimes settle into awkward silence simply because neither person has anything more to add to the topic. Reigniting a conversation can be as simple as picking one point earlier in the discussion to expound on by sharing facts or trivia.

For example, say you were discussing moving back to the city after your kids leave for college. "Since moving to New York five years ago, I've never missed the annual St. Patrick's Day parade in Manhattan. Did you know that the coronavirus pandemic in 2020 caused the celebration to be postponed for the first time in over 250 years?"

"I'm definitely moving back to New York after the twins leave for college in September. I love Manhattan, but I'm actually thinking about getting a place on the Brooklyn waterfront. Instead of living on the island, I can have a great view of it."

Or you can continue the conversation at the last point before the awkward silence. "Taking my son to visit colleges brought back so many great memories of being a college student. You could always find me in the museum sketching. I always lost track of time in there."

A tactic that I like to use to break silences is offering or asking for an opinion about a current shared experience. It should be something that engages one or more of the five senses. You might comment on the food: "These are the best tomatoes I've tasted in a long time. And their color is so vibrant." Or you might ask about the music: "Guitar music is my favorite. Weren't you blown away by that solo?"

## Stay Civil

Valerie is a mother who has volunteered to lead the bake sale at her son's new school. She's just started a conversation with Pytor, who has a daughter in the same class.

**Pytor:** How do you like the neighborhood?

**Valerie:** Oh, it's great! So much to explore. It's only our third week here.

**Pytor:** You'll love it here. If you have any questions, let me know.

**Valerie:** My son needs a bike. We were going to the check out the store on Canary Street.

**Pytor:** No, don't go there. I heard that the owner Ralph doesn't believe in soap.

**Valerie:** Doesn't believe in soap?

**Pytor:** He doesn't believe in it. Never uses it. Water and wipe only. For everything.

**Valerie:** That's . . . odd?

**Pytor:** No soap. Not for washing his hands. Not for doing the dishes.

**Valerie:** Okay, maybe we'll go to another store.

**Pytor:** Can you imagine how dirty his kitchen must be?

**Valerie:** Would you recommend the bicycle shop on Beeton Road?

**Pytor:** How does he wash his clothes without soap?

**Valerie:** The bicycle shop on Beeton Road had solid reviews online.

**Pytor:** Sorry, I shouldn't gossip. It just boggles the mind.

**Valerie:** It is curious, but let's not speculate.

**Pytor:** You're right. Yes, the Beeton Road shop is great. I just bought bikes for my entire family there. If you buy two or more bikes, they'll give you helmets for free.

**Valerie:** Good to know. Thanks.

In this conversation, Pytor let himself get swept away in gossip about Ralph. Rather than participating in unfounded gossip, Valerie twice turns Pytor's attention to another bicycle shop. Since they are parents with children in the same class, they will inevitably cross paths in the future, so Valerie is careful to keep the discussion civil.

# Avoid Conversation Killers

Certain behaviors will lead to awkward silences or kill conversations altogether. Avoid the following:

**Being contrary to display dominance or just for the sake of argument.** Most people will find it unpleasant to be in a conversation where every comment they make is contradicted. If you are arguing everything that is being said, you are not actively listening—you are debating.

**Making everything about you.** People want to be heard. If you listen only to the point where you can turn the attention to you, you are not empathizing. You might think you are relating, but you will simply come across as narcissistic.

**Offering unsolicited advice.** This is especially frustrating when it's given before the person is even done explaining their situation. Let the other person finish their story and only offer your thoughts if the person asks for them after confiding in you. Don't be so arrogant to assume everyone needs your wisdom.

**Constantly interrupting.** It's rude and makes you look like an impatient child who can't wait their turn to speak. Yes, it's great that you're excited to interact, but it's not great that you cannot control your impulse to cut the other person off all the time. It also breaks the flow of conversation.

# Bounce Back from a Misstep

Conversational blunders will happen. They're almost unavoidable, so just be prepared for them if you catch yourself committing one. Here are several ways to bounce back from a misstep.

## Don't be overly contradictory

If you are contradicting every remark the other person makes just for the sake of argument, you're creating an environment that is unpleasant at best and hostile at worst. Stop yourself and reassure the person you will be making a more concerted effort to listen. "I apologize. I realize I may have been looking at things from a different vantage point. Please let me try to see things from your perspective."

## Empathize by focusing on the other person

If you make everything about you, people don't feel heard. Empathize instead of responding with your own examples. "I'm sorry. I didn't mean to redirect the focus to me. This conversation is about you, and I won't react with my own stories."

## Don't offer advice until asked

Unsolicited advice is especially frustrating for people who haven't even finished speaking. Let others complete their thoughts and give them the chance to ask for your response. Maybe they just want someone to listen to them. If you really think they would benefit from your advice, ask if they would welcome it after confiding in you. "Thank you for sharing your situation with me. Would you like my advice on the matter, or did you just want someone to listen to your story?"

## Listen fully and wait to speak

Constant interruptions are rude and break the flow of conversation. Wait your turn to speak so you don't come across as impulsive and impatient. "Apologies for my interruptions. This conversation makes my mind race with thoughts I want to share, but I'll be more mindful about listening to you fully first."

Everyone makes these mistakes on occasion; just don't let them become a habit. When you find yourself detracting from the conversation, pause and wait for an appropriate moment to apologize. You can gracefully save a conversation from minor gaffes.

# Transition Away from Uncomfortable Topics

There will be people who overstep boundaries because they don't have the awareness to know they are being intrusive. Still others will do so intentionally because they want to pry. Here are tactics you can use to transition away from uncomfortable topics.

**Make a question about you into a broad statement,** then follow with a general question about your redirected focus. For example, a lot of people are comfortable talking about their jobs, but not their salaries. If someone asks a tailor how much he makes, he might respond, "Every project is different, but I've had a few good years recently because our sales team has been bringing in more clients. Overall, morale has been improved. Have you found the same in your company now that consumers are more interested in sustainable farming?"

**Simply change the topic.** You don't have to answer every question asked of you or reply to every comment directed at you. In fact, sometimes it's better not to engage in certain topics at all. If someone is making you uncomfortable in a conversation but you can't just end it, talk about something else that you can both be positive about. "I really admire how much thought was put into today's programming. The planning committee did an exemplary job."

**Be direct.** Directly tell the other person you don't want to discuss the topic they've brought up. You don't need to be rude or dramatic about it, but be firm. You can simply let them know you'd rather discuss something else and offer up a new topic for conversation.

### Don't be Inappropriate or Rude

Unfortunately, gossip is a quick way for people to bond—especially if it's negative. Don't make conversation at another person's expense. At the very least, you never know if you might want that person as a friend or ally in the future.

Ellen and Hamadi have been friends for the past three years. They have a close relationship, but Hamadi still manages to be inappropriate or overstep the boundaries sometimes. He often uses rude criticism to open a conversation, but that's never a good strategy. Here's a conversation they had after a cross training class:

Hamadi: Did you see the woman in the orange outfit? Her leggings were at least two sizes too small.

Ellen: We're not here for a fashion show. I liked the new instructor's pace. What did you think?

**Hamadi:** I think orange outfit girl needs a mirror. Does she not see the fabric bursting at the seams?

**Ellen:** And I think you need to redirect your attention to the class we paid for.

**Hamadi:** C'mon, you're always impeccably dressed. That girl is delusional if she thinks she looks good.

**Ellen:** It's time to change the subject. How is your parents' kitchen renovation progressing?

**Hamadi:** Okay, I get it. I'll stop it with the fashion policing. The kitchen is almost done. They just need to have drawers installed under the new sink.

Just as Hamadi is naturally gossipy, Ellen is naturally kind. Be like Ellen. If someone makes a rude comment, change the focus of the conversation and follow with a relevant question. If the person doesn't take that hint, try again and more explicitly. If all else fails, politely but directly tell the person that you will not engage in such conversation. If you're gracious, help the other person out by suggesting a new topic to discuss.

# Spice up a Boring Conversation

Some topics are likely to lead to mundane chit-chat. Unless you're a meteorologist, how much can you really say about the weather? If a conversation starts to become dull or boring, look for clues about things that the other person finds exciting. Do they have framed prints on their walls of pirate ships or military helicopters? Is their home or office filled with artifacts from their international travels? Do they spend a lot of time volunteering for certain causes?

> If a conversation starts to become dull or boring, look for clues about things that the other person finds exciting.

If you don't have clues specific to what the other person enjoys talking about, you can always turn to safe, dependable topics such as popular entertainment, music, movies, and food. Start off general and let their responses help guide the rest of the conversation. Even if you begin talking about a topic that they have no interest in, you can turn the conversation from there. I met someone who never listened to contemporary music growing up. They didn't have the same cultural reference points as I did, but I used that moment to ask them what they did listen to instead. From there, I learned about their love of very early jazz, picked up from their parents' musical preferences.

## Recognize Boundaries and Recover Gracefully

Here's a conversation that covers some of the ideas in this chapter:

**Chevohn:** I love your outfit! You're always so stylish, but I don't know how you can afford it!

**Heather:** Thank you. My brother is a fashion designer, so he often gives me tips.

**Chevohn:** You must make good money as a CPA! Your sunglasses alone cost more than my entire outfit.

**Heather:** I prefer not to discuss my personal finances. Isn't the weather great today?

**Chevohn:** Yes.

**Heather:** I heard it's going to rain tomorrow, so I'll be going to the movies. Do you recommend any of the ones that just hit the theaters?

**Chevohn:** Definitely go see the new movie about the haunted castles. It's fantastic! I've seen it three times already. Based on a true story! The book is even better.

**Heather:** I didn't know the movie was based on a true story. My brother—

**Chevohn:** You should definitely read the fan fiction online, too. There is this Swiss writer . . . I'm so sorry! I am really a huge fan of this movie, and I didn't mean to interrupt you. You were saying that your brother?

**Heather:** I was saying that my brother lent me his copy of the book and I'm reading it this weekend. No need to apologize. Please tell me about the Swiss writer.

Sometimes, you may not recognize other people's boundaries because they are being polite and answering you vaguely with a smile. If you realize you overstepped, don't just awkwardly stall the conversation with curt responses because you suddenly feel bad. Instead, change the subject and keep the conversation lively. One faux pas doesn't have to kill a discussion. Always try to end on a positive note, on your terms, not because you inappropriately blundered and want to run away.

# Remember This

- Unless you have a solid personal relationship with someone, it's prudent to avoid conversations that are religious or political. Avoid making comments that are racist, sexist, or ethnically insensitive.

- If you find yourself killing a conversation or committing a misstep, just pause and recover as gracefully as possible. Apologize and acknowledge your faux pas.

- The best way to save a conversation is to stay aware of yourself and the other person. Actively listen so that when you steer a discussion in the direction you want it to go in, you are mindful of the other person's interests and goals.

## CHAPTER EIGHT

# CLOSE GRACEFULLY

Gracefully ending a conversation is an art, and it's important for leaving a lasting impression. You want to start and end a conversation strong, in such a way that the other person remembers you in a positive light.

Don't wait until you reach a point of awkward silence where neither of you has anything more to add to the discussion. It's also not great to just stop talking abruptly and say, "Okay, goodbye!" before you scurry away.

The best way to close a conversation is a smooth transition. Look for closing signs and wrap up the conversation nicely. If you'd like to speak with the other person again, exchange contact information.

# Look for Closing Signs

A good conversationalist is able to read signs that it's time to close a conversation. Verbally, the other person will slow down their rate of engagement. They will ask fewer questions and give shorter answers. They are mentally checking out, so if you had a good discussion up to this point, it's best to end the discussion before it gets too awkward and painful.

Nonverbal cues that let you know you should start winding down to a close in the conversation include:

**Yawning.** This is obvious. The other person is no longer excited about talking to you.

**Breaking eye contact.** Their eyes are no longer focused on you but are wandering the room. They're more interested in what's happening around or behind you.

**Distancing.** The other person moves their body away from yours. Their feet are pointed at the door.

**Fidgeting.** They are tapping their fingers or toes. They're impatient and anxious to end the conversation with you.

**Checking their watch or phone.** The other person is concerned with the next thing they will be doing. They are not fully invested in their time with you.

If you see any of these cues to close a conversation, do so. Give yourself or the other person a polite and plausible reason to leave.

## Appreciate People for Their Time, If Not Their Conversation

Luke sat down at the picnic table and looked over an enormous bowl of potato salad to find a man wearing a shirt with the German flag on it. He smiled and introduced himself, "Hi,

I'm Luke, Carmen's brother. Nice shirt—I've always wanted to visit Germany."

"I'm Carl. I'm the brother of Carmen's boss," the man responded. "I've never been to Germany. Or anywhere outside of this town, actually. I hate traveling. My nephew gave me this shirt from his semester abroad."

As an avid traveler, Luke fought to hide his disappointment. He changed the topic to ask Carl what he did for a living and learned that Carl sold timeshares to luxury condos 20 minutes from the park. While Luke had absolutely no interest in time-shares, he still actively listened and asked relevant questions. Luke waited for at least 10 minutes for someone to join in and change the group dynamic, but no one did. Carl refused to talk about anything else and even started trying to sell Luke a unit. Given Carl's connection to his sister, Luke had to remain civil at the very least while he patiently listened to the long sales pitch. When Carl was done, Luke smiled and said, "Thank you so much for your time, Carl. Our conversation was very informative. I'll keep you in mind if I ever need a timeshare. Now, though, I really need to help Carmen with the cooking."

# Wrap it Up Nicely

If you are ready to end a conversation, do so in a way that doesn't make the other person feel uncomfortable or unwanted. Nonverbally, you can subtly move your body away from the other person. Lean back in your chair if you're sitting. Point your feet toward the door if you're standing.

Verbally, you might signal the end of the conversation with one of the following statements:

- I enjoyed our conversation. Thank you for sharing your time with me.

  (Polite and ends on a nice note.)

- I would like to meet another new person here. Who would you suggest I speak with next?

    (If you're at an event, the person you're speaking with might even proactively connect you with the next person.)

- Given what you've told me, I think you'd really like to meet my friend/colleague. Would you like me to introduce you?

    (This gives you an opportunity to help others.)

- Will you be at the next meeting? I'd like to continue our conversation then.

    (Signals to the other person that you would like to speak with them again.)

- I'd like to keep in touch. May I ask for your contact information?

    (Lets the other person know you may try to reach out to them at a later time.)

## Try Not to End Conversations Abruptly

Different exits will yield different outcomes. See what happens when Tom ends a conversation at an event abruptly rather than wrapping things up properly.

**Scenario A:**

Osman: That's why I decided to send my children to the music school across town.

Tom: Great. Thanks. Good to know. Okay, bye.

In this scenario, Osman is blindsided by Tom's sudden departure. Osman feels unwanted and uncomfortable about the exchange he just had with Tom. He doesn't initiate contact with Tom in the future even when they cross paths again.

**Scenario B:**

**Osman:** That's why I decided to send my children to the music school across town.

**Tom:** I understand why you would make that decision. I would have done the same.

**Osman:** Right? The alternative just doesn't make any sense.

**Tom:** I need to leave in 20 minutes, but I'd like to meet one more new person before doing so. Know anyone else I should speak with?

**Osman:** I know just the guy. Warren is my tax attorney. He just bought a new house in the next town over and needs a landscaper. Definitely show him the photos you showed me of the garden you designed last year.

**Tom:** Thank so much. And here's my card. Just text me when you want to join me for beach volleyball. The season starts next week.

In this alternate scenario, Tom's active listening and feedback make Osman feel heard and understood. Osman feels positive about the interaction, and this is reinforced by Tom's offer to meet again for a leisure activity. Osman makes an introduction to Warren, who then becomes Tom's biggest client. Everyone wins.

# Hand It Off

I'm a big fan of handing off a conversation by introducing someone new, because I've helped two people connect and I don't feel like I'm abandoning anyone. The best way to do this is by highlighting why the other two people might be interested in speaking with one another.

For example, if I were introducing Tom to Warren, I'd begin by giving context. I met Tom when I was volunteering at last week's fundraiser for autistic children. Tom showed me photos of a koi-themed garden he designed last year. I was impressed by his attention to detail. Then, I'd introduce him to Warren, repeating that Warren had just bought a new house in the next town over. This way, both men know why I think they should talk to each other. I've already set the stage for them to connect. Maybe they'll talk about landscaping or maybe they'll change topics quickly. Either way, I can make an exit by saying, "Unfortunately, I can't stay and chat longer. I need to leave, but it was great seeing both of you. Enjoy the rest of the event."

If possible, always try to provide context when you are introducing someone new into a conversation. This gives others information to work off of and draw in the new person more effectively.

# Make Connections

As you read in the scenario with Tom and Osman, sometimes the most valuable offer you can give someone is an introduction. There, Osman was able to provide the context for the introduction in person. If you are thinking about connecting two people virtually, first make sure both individuals are open to the suggestion. After you have gotten the green light to make the connection, you can write one succinct email to both with the following information:

**Offer introductions for those who don't know each other.** Explain how you know the two people you are trying to connect. Provide context such as, "I've known Sohwon since college. We were on the cross-country ski team together." The longevity of your relationship with Sohwon offers assurance that you're not sending along a stranger you just met. Sohwon is someone you spent a significant amount of time with in college and have maintained contact with after graduating.

**Provide value-add details for the suggestion to connect.** Explain why you think this connection is mutually beneficial. "Sohwon would be a great asset to your run for mayor because she has worked on successful political campaigns for three senators. She is incredibly media savvy, and she currently has a seat open on the Board of her engineering company. It's a serendipitous opportunity for you to advise her team with your NASA experience in exchange for the media training you need."

# Exchange Information

If you had a great conversation with someone, it's natural to want to stay in touch and speak with them again. Exchanging contact information is usually straightforward and direct in business settings. Before mobile phones could easily handle email, you'd exchange business cards and follow up with a note sent from the desktop in your office. Cards are easily lost, though, and people can forget why they planned to connect. These days, it's not uncommon to send an email from your phone right after speaking with someone. That way, they'll have your email already in their inbox with reminders about the conversation. Just send a quick note that includes where you met and what you spoke about at the time. It can be as simple as, "Hi Daria. It was great meeting you at the artificial intelligence conference in San Francisco. I'd love to set up a call next week to discuss the new software you're presenting to Google. Thanks. Regards, Craig." A message like this is more likely to trigger a response than just giving someone your email or phone number on a slip of paper.

Social settings get more complicated because everyone wants varying degrees of privacy and connectedness. The safest approach is to simply offer your contact information and invite them to message you. If you feel this approach is too forward or assuming, you may ask how you might send them a message to stay in touch. This alternative strategy is helpful because some people have very specific channels they want to use for keeping in touch. For instance, you may like texting, but many of the younger generations prefer messaging on social media platforms.

If someone declines to provide you with their information, don't press the matter. They are not interested in being contacted and you should definitely let them keep their privacy. Don't search for them online or send any messages after the conversation has ended.

# Set up Future Conversations

Setting up future conversations can be tricky. You want to be accommodating but not pushy or overeager. Here are three approaches you can try:

**Very casual.** "I enjoyed our conversation. How about getting coffee next week?" This invitation is very light and good for when you want to gauge the other person's interest without looking overeager.

**Casual.** "It was great meeting you. Let's get lunch next week. Maybe Wednesday at 1:00 pm?" This approach can be used when you're fairly certain the other person would be interested in meeting again, and it shows your level of commitment. You're suggesting lunch, which takes more time than a cup of coffee, and you're providing a specific day and time to meet.

**Business.** "I'd like to set up a meeting to discuss hiring your team to build the wheelchair-accessible entrance. I'm free all next week after 3:00 pm. Our office is on 31 North Main Street." As usual, the business example is the most straightforward. You are telling the other person why you would like to speak again, when you are available so they can check against their own schedule, and where you are located so they can plan their commute.

In each of these examples, the best outcome would be another positive interaction. However, be prepared for some people to accept but never actually follow through to speak again because they are not interested or they are too busy. Some won't even reply at all. In the latter two cases, you can reach out a second time just in case your first note got lost in the shuffle of life. Very rarely should you ping someone more than three times without a response.

# Excuse Yourself Politely

As much as possible, wrap up your conversations nicely to leave a positive impression. You might not think a discussion went well, but it may have been because of a reason unrelated to you. Maybe the other person already had a stressful day before speaking with you. Maybe the other person didn't feel well physically. If you leave a conversation on a good note, it increases the chances that the other person will want to speak with you again when they are feeling better. If you leave rudely, you're just making the situation unpleasant and ruining your chances of a follow-up.

Here are some phrases you can use to excuse yourself politely:

- It looks like my team needs some assistance. I'm going to head over there to offer a helping hand.

- Thank you so much for your time—I won't take up any more of it right now so you can speak with other people.

- I know you're busy, so I'll let you get back to your work. It was a pleasure speaking with you.

- The next speaker will begin soon, and I need to send an email to the office before they go on stage. Please excuse me.

- I enjoyed our conversation. Thank you. I'm going to refresh my drink.

## Make Positivity and Politeness Your Default

You will never be rewarded for rudeness, so try to be polite and positive no matter the circumstances. See what happens when Kayla takes offense at Nang's distracted conversation below:

**Scenario A:**

Nang: I'm sorry. Can you tell me again how to get to the museum?

Kayla: You seem very distracted. It's probably better for you to just search online for the route than for you to try remembering what I tell you again.

Nang: Well, okay. Thanks.

Now, imagine if Kayla used more polite positivity:

**Scenario B:**

Nang: I'm sorry. Can you tell me again how to get to the museum?

Kayla: You were just in a car accident with your son. It's understandable to be distracted!

Nang: I really dislike asking people to repeat themselves.

Kayla: No one is at 100 percent all the time. Here, I'll write the directions on this napkin for you.

Nang: This is super kind of you. I really appreciate it. We're taking my daughter to the museum tomorrow, then the opera on Sunday.

**Kayla:** Lucky girl! I love the opera.

**Nang:** Would you like my son's ticket? He can no longer attend, so we have an extra seat.

**Kayla:** That's so generous of you. Thank you!

**Nang:** You've been so patient with me. It's the least I can do.

**Kayla:** I'm always happy to help when I can. In fact, my team over there looks like they need a little assistance. I'm going to head over to help them arrange the books, but I look forward to chatting again on Sunday.

# Remember This

- Always remain polite and positive. Sometimes people are just having bad days unrelated to you.

- Close gracefully when a conversation has reached a natural ending. Offer to exchange contact information, but don't be pushy about it.

- Look for opportunities to connect people in your network even if it doesn't seem to immediately benefit you. Making introductions for others is a valuable service that may help you in the future.

CHAPTER NINE
# PRACTICE

Small talk skills develop with time and practice. I've been honing my skills for over a decade and I am still surprised on a regular basis. Little interactions can produce large results. You don't know where a friendly chat may take you because everyone is connected to part of a different community.

I urge you to talk to people from many diverse networks. Talk to the CEO. Talk to your nephew. Talk to the stranger in the coffee shop.

As industry leader and 2013 *Forbes* Magazine Top 15 Social Media Power Influencer Ted Rubin explains, "Relationships are like muscle tissue . . . the more they're engaged, the stronger and more valuable they become."

# Professional Networking

Before you attend a professional networking event, do research about the speakers and attendees and be clear about your goals. Do you want to meet thought leaders to co-author articles for publication? Are you looking for a job? Do you want to find investors for your company? Are you looking to sell more product? You should have a tailored pitch for each goal because you will be emphasizing different aspects depending on the person you're engaging.

Using the possible goals above, here are examples of some things you might say:

**Co-authoring:** "I read your three most recent stories about diversity in the workplace. I even used your research on Goldman Sachs for the entrepreneurship class I teach. I'm currently working on an article for *Harvard Business Review* and I'd love to see if you're interested in co-authoring with me."

**Employment:** "Your company website does a phenomenal job of explaining how it recruits international engineers. The statistics are impressive, especially in Europe. I'm from Zurich, and I wonder if you know anything about the database architect job listed on the careers page?"

**Investors:** "The mission statement for your company mentions corporate social responsibility, and I'm interested in knowing more because I'm currently leading a nonprofit to support art education in underprivileged neighborhoods in the state. I'd like to suggest a way we can work together that benefits us both."

# Dating

It's always a good idea to be prepared with conversation starters, but be careful not to barrage your dates with a list a questions. Talk a little about yourself between questions so your date gets to learn about you, too. Maintain a balance of learning about one another. Some good topics to discuss include:

**Personal interest projects.** A lot of people would rather not discuss their jobs during dates, but they're happy to chat about how they spend their free time. You might hear about a skateboarding hobby or a competitive robotics demonstration. Their answer can tell you how invested they are in their projects and if they have time for you in their lives.

**Vacation style.** This conversation is a favorite topic of mine because I cannot date anyone with incompatible preferences for how we might spend holidays. For example, I have absolutely no interest in taking a motorcycle ride across the country or backpacking in the mountains. He might despise my idea to visit famous museums in Europe and attend the annual wristwatch show in Basel, Switzerland. It would also be difficult for me to date someone who likes to start the day early and follow a rigid schedule while traveling.

**Pets/Animals.** Many people are very emotional or at least opinionated about pets. There's even a movie about it, *Must Love Dogs*. Pets and animals are good for conversation because there's no correct answer, but you can discover more about your compatibility. If your date has two dogs but you're highly allergic, that person may not be the one for you.

Find topics of conversation where you can check if you are compatible with your date. You don't have to match exactly, but it's important to know if you're willing to negotiate and compromise where you differ. You can also find out how you might learn something new from one another or grow together. Maybe the person is a kitesurfing expert and you've always wanted to try out that sport.

# Weddings and Family Events

Because everyone at a wedding is invited by someone connected to the couple being married, an easy first question is, "Who do you know in the wedding party?" You should be prepared to answer this question as well. It would be great if you have an uplifting story about the couple to share, like how they met on a rainy camping trip in college or volunteering at an animal shelter. People like hearing stories about mutual connections, and it's a quick way to bond.

If you were invited as a "plus one" guest to a wedding or family gathering and you don't have any stories to share, ask for one. "Do you know how the couple met?" "I wonder why she chose a Hawaiian theme for her birthday celebration?" "Do you have any funny stories about the college graduate?"

Or you can ask similar questions about the other person. "How did you meet your spouse?" "What theme would you have chosen for your milestone birthday?" "What's the most memorable thing you did after graduating from college?" Use active listening to ask relevant follow-up questions and be prepared to be asked the same questions.

# Casual Get-Togethers

Less formal get-togethers such as happy hour, picnics, and BBQs make casual conversation easier. People are more open to friendly chats. I usually open by asking how they are enjoying the event, because most people will answer positively and add a little bit of information I can follow-up on. For example, they might answer, "This picnic is great. I haven't seen my nephews since they moved out-of-state. I'm also looking forward to the start of beach volleyball season." You can then respond by asking open-ended questions that require more than a yes or no:

- Where did your nephews move to? How long have they been there and how do they like it?

- When does the season start? Do you play?

If the other person doesn't add much information to their answer, you should give them a positive suggestion or mention something else particular to the get-together, such as:

- Have you visited the dessert table? I just had the carrot cake and it's delicious.

- Are you planning to go swimming later? The rope swing brings back so many great memories from my college days as a lifeguard.

Casual get-togethers are good for starting conversations about your shared experiences. Are you eating the same foods, trying the same drinks, or playing the same games? People are there to have fun and socialize, so they will be more open to conversation.

# Out and About

When you're out and about, such as when you're grocery shopping, traveling, or attending a concert, the ease of starting and maintaining a conversation will be less predictable. There will be people who won't want to talk to you. Don't take it personally. Maybe they've had a long day, maybe they don't like talking to strangers, or maybe they're just shy. Or maybe they simply don't have time for chatting. Not everyone likes connecting to others when they are just going about their day and completing tasks.

Generally, I begin with eye contact and a smile to the person I'm planning to engage in conversation. Hopefully, they reciprocate so I clearly know they are open to talking to me. I usually start with a light opinion about our shared environment because it gives them an easy way to respond. They can agree or disagree with me. Most people are very quick to give opinions. Here are some examples for what to say in different locales.

- **At the grocery store:** "I like the new pricing labels. They are so much easier to read and understand."

- **At the airport:** "I'm so glad they moved the water fountain to the other side of the building. The foot traffic moves so much quicker now."

- **At a concert:** "These new seats are so much more comfortable, and the fabric is beautiful."

Or reframed as questions:

- **At the grocery store:** "Do you like the new pricing labels? I find them so much easier to read and understand."

- **At the airport:** "Aren't you glad the water fountain has been moved to the other side of the building? The foot traffic moves so much quicker now."

- **At a concert:** "Do you find the new seats more comfortable?"

## Real-Life Scenarios

Here are some tips on how to engage in various real-life scenarios:

**Situation:** You go to a party where you don't know anyone except the host.

**Advice:** Ask the host if there's anything you can do to help. I often volunteer to bartend because everyone talks to the bartender. Some questions you might ask:
- How do you know the host?
- Who else have you met so far?
- Is there anything I can do to make this party better for you?

**Situation:** You're a guest at a wedding and your date leaves you at the table to catch up with friends.

**Advice:** Get to know the other people at the table. Some questions you might ask:
- How are you connected to the couple?
- Do you know how the couple met?
- Who else do you know at this wedding?

**Situation:** You have to take a new employee out to lunch.

**Advice:** Make the new employee feel like they are welcome to the company and that you are happy to be a resource. Some things you might say:
- Let me know if there's anything you need.
- Feel free to reach out to me if you have any questions.
- What interested you about joining this company?
- What are some of the projects you will be working on?
- Have you been surprised by anything so far?

**Situation:** You're in a bad mood on a plane and the passenger next to you is trying to engage with you.

**Advice:** I don't always think you should make conversation every time an opportunity presents itself, because being in a bad mood may mean you make an undesirable impression. A lack of impression is better than a bad one. To avoid having a conversation with the passenger next to you who is trying to engage, you can simply say, "I'm sorry. Normally, I'd love to talk to you, but I'm afraid I wouldn't be very good company right now."

There have been times when I pushed myself through a bad mood just to be polite, and it paid off because the other person lifted my spirits with laughter or helped me

→

resolve the reason I wasn't in a great mood. You might say a version of the statement above but end with details about what put you in a funk. For example, "I'm sorry. Normally, I'd love to talk to you, but I'm afraid I wouldn't be very good company right now because I just found out that my business partner no longer has the funds to invest in our start-up." It's very possible that the stranger would be interested in investing in your start-up or know others who would. You don't know what is possible until you verbalize your needs.

# Remember This

- Be prepared, especially in business settings. This will help you avoid awkward silences and will signal to the other person you have invested time in speaking with them.

- Be aware of your surroundings so you can talk about shared experiences.

- Aim to keep a good balance of exchanging information with the other person. Ask questions about them so they speak at least 60 percent of the time.

# CLOSING

The lessons in this book should serve as a navigational tool for improving your conversation skills. The most important factor for becoming better at connecting with others is practice. Talk to everyone, not just those in your network or those who are similar to you. The more diverse the range of people you speak with, the stronger you make your abilities.

Being good at small talk takes practice and time. Don't get frustrated if your improvement is not immediate. After a decade, I'm still honing my skills.

For every conversation, keep in mind:

1. Be ready to contribute to conversations with insight, positivity, and resources. Offer before you take. Always add value to discussions.

2. Keep an open mind and be empathetic. Don't allow your first impressions to determine who you choose to engage in a discussion. You might be pleasantly surprised!

3. Maintain a good balance of eye contact. Practice good posture and hold your body with confidence. Subtly mirror gestures and expressions.

4. Show that you appreciate the time others are willing to give you. Make them feel heard and valued for their conversation.

5. Listen actively and fully to what the other person is saying, not just to what you want to hear. Try to empathize with the other person and understand their perspective, given their history and experiences.

6. Deepen the conversation by expressing your curiosity and asking meaningful follow-up questions based on what you hear. Navigate the conversation in a way that makes it flow naturally.

7. Don't rely on a script of what you plan to say.

8. Paraphrase for clarity. Don't make assumptions.

9. Be genuine, specific, and succinct about your compliments. Recognize others for their accomplishments.

10. Don't just complain about problems; work toward finding solutions for them. Give people reasons to gravitate toward you instead of away from you.

11. Incorporate stories that are memorable, captivating, and engaging. Use details to connect emotionally and build rapport.

12. Unless you have a solid personal relationship with someone, avoid conversations that are religious or political. Don't make comments or jokes that are racist, sexist, or ethnically insensitive.

13. Always remain polite and positive. Sometimes people are just having bad days unrelated to you.

Learning to connect meaningfully with others is one of the best investments you can make in yourself, personally and professionally. You've made a wonderful decision! I wish you luck in your endeavors.

# RESOURCES

Two thought leaders I highly recommend you read and follow:

**Dorie Clark (DorieClark.com)**
Dorie is a branding expert recognized by *Fortune*, the Associated Press, and *Inc.* magazine. The *New York Times* calls her an "expert at self-reinvention and helping others make changes in their lives." She is excellent at teaching others how to present themselves and stand out, especially in business settings.

A frequent contributor to the *Harvard Business Review*, Dorie is also the author of *Entrepreneurial You* (Harvard Business Review Press) and *Reinventing You*. Her first book, *Stand Out*, was ranked the #1 Leadership Book of 2015 by *Inc.* magazine and one of the Top 10 Business Books of the Year by *Forbes*. It was also a *Washington Post* bestseller.

**Ted Rubin (TedRubin.com)**
Ted Rubin is a social media strategist and keynote speaker. *Forbes* Magazine ranked him among the Top 15 Social Media Power Influencers in 2013. The Photofy CMO is an expert in community-building, based on the concept of Return on Relationship™, #RonR. He has authored two books that are relevant to connecting with others: *Return on Relationship*, released in January 2013, and *How To Look People in the Eye Digitally*, released in January 2015.

# REFERENCES

CHAPTER ONE
Gibbons, Serenity. "You And Your Business Have 7 Seconds To Make A First Impression: Here's How To Succeed." *Forbes*, June 20, 2018. Forbes.com/sites/serenitygibbons/2018/06/19/you-have-7-seconds -to-make-a-first-impression-heres-how-to-succeed.

CHAPTER TWO
Cuncic, Arlin. "How to Overcome Eye Contact Anxiety." Verywell Mind, December 5, 2019. VerywellMind.com/how-do-i-maintain-good-eye-contact-3024392.

McGregor, Jena, and Shelly Tan. "What to Do with Your Hands When Speaking in Public." *The Washington Post*. WP Company, November 17, 2015. WashingtonPost.com/news/on-leadership/ wp/2015/11/17/what-to-do-with-your-hands-when-speaking -in-public.

CHAPTER THREE
Blaschka, Amy. "Five Hard Truths About Soft Skills That Might Surprise You." *Forbes*, April 12, 2019. Forbes.com/ sites/amyblaschka/2019/04/11/five-surprisingly-hard-truths -about-soft-skills.

CHAPTER FIVE
Washington, Ella F., Alison Hall Birch, and Laura Morgan Roberts. "When and How to Respond to Microaggressions." *Harvard Business Review*. Harvard Business School Publishing, July 3, 2020. HBR.org /2020/07/when-and-how-to-respond-to-microaggressions.

## CHAPTER SIX
Klein, Christopher. "How Prohibition Gave Birth to NASCAR."
The History Channel, November 17, 2017. History.com/news/how
-prohibition-gave-birth-to-nascar.

Podhoretz, Jim, dir. *30 for 30*. Season 3, Episode 16, "Celtics/Lakers:
Best of Enemies, Part 1." Aired June 13, 2017. ESPN.

Williams, Ray. "Are You a Mindful Leader?" *Financial Post*, May 23,
2013. business.FinancialPost.com/executive/careers/are-you-a
-mindful-leader.

## CHAPTER NINE
Rubin, Ted. "Relationships Are Like Muscle Tissue…". Ted Rubin,
November 5, 2017. TedRubin.com/relationships-like-muscle-tissue/.

## RESOURCES
Brody, Jane E. "Reinventing Yourself." *The New York Times*, March 14,
2016. well.blogs.NYtimes.com/2016/03/14/reinventing-yourself/.

# INDEX

# ACKNOWLEDGMENTS

I offer deep gratitude to my Dartmouth College family, with special mention to Joan Ai; Dr. Alli Giordano; Aryeh Drager, PhD; Joseph Furlett, Esq.; Barrett Weeks; Sue Reed; Charles H. Allison Jr.; Lancel Joseph; Bill Greenbaum; Bryant Prieur; Mark Caron; Shaun Akhtar; and Heather Stocks Pixley. Thank you to the Phi Tau Brotherhood for weekly calls while I wrote this book during the 2020 quarantine.

Much appreciation to my friends Stephen Earl Bates; Michael Kannisto, PhD; Thomas White; Brian D'Amato; Dr. Enoch Choi; Angela Maiers; Richard Levangie; Michael S. Kelly; David Towber; Cameron Villers; Daniel Ramirez-Raftree; Timothy McDonald; Ben Villa; and Joe Barbagallo.

This book would not have been possible without all of you, plus the wonderful team at Callisto Media, with special acknowledgement to my patient editors Brian Sweeting and John Makowski. THANK YOU SO MUCH!

# ABOUT THE AUTHOR

 **Lisa Chau** is the creator of the TED-Ed lesson *Networking for the Networking Averse*, which as of this writing has been viewed over 160,000 times. Her writing has been featured in *Forbes, Buzzfeed, Thrive Global, US News & World Report*, and *Huffington Post* on TABLES: Technology - Academia - Business - Leadership - Entrepreneurship - Strategy. Her work includes profiling high-level executives, successful entrepreneurs, established professors, distinguished creatives, and award-winning authors.

She was a featured guest on "Midday with Dan Roderick," speaking on millennials and digital strategy. The show aired on National Public Radio (NPR) Baltimore.

At MIT, Lisa led a seven-week summer course for high schoolers explaining how to use social media to enhance professional networking. Lisa has also lectured undergraduates and MBA candidates at The New School and The Zicklin School of Business at Baruch College. Smith College invited her to speak as a part of their Executive Education Leadership Series. With Fu Foundation School of Engineering at Columbia alumnus Canberk Dayan, Lisa co-organized and co-hosted the How to Build a Strong Start-Up Conference at Columbia University, mentioned in Yahoo Finance.

Lisa has spoken on multiple Ivy League campuses, including Yale, Princeton, and her alma mater, Dartmouth College. She is a passionate alumna who served on the Board of the Dartmouth College Club of the Upper Valley and continues to serve on the Board of the Dartmouth College Club of New York.

In conjunction with this book, Lisa began accepting international private clients to develop tailored professional strategies designed to empower their careers and showcase their leadership. Connect with Lisa via CloverCanal2020.wordpress.com.

CPSIA information can be obtained
at www.ICGtesting.com
Printed in the USA
LVHW010738201120
672161LV00002B/2